UNDERSTANDING AND LOVING A PERSON WITH

BIPOLAR DISORDER

UNDERSTANDING AND LOVING A PERSON WITH

BIPOLAR DISORDER

*Biblical and Practical Wisdom
to Build Empathy, Preserve Boundaries,
and Show Compassion*

STEPHEN ARTERBURN, M.Ed.
AND BECKY LYKE BROWN, M.S.

DAVID C COOK

transforming lives together

UNDERSTANDING AND LOVING A PERSON WITH BIPOLAR DISORDER
Published by David C Cook
4050 Lee Vance Drive
Colorado Springs, CO 80918 U.S.A.

Integrity Music Limited, a Division of David C Cook
Eastbourne, East Sussex BN23 6NT, England

The graphic circle C logo is a registered trademark of David C Cook.

LCCN 2017964689
ISBN 978-0-7814-1492-0
eISBN 978-0-8307-7273-5

Cover Design: Amy Konyndyk

Printed in the United States of America
First Edition 2018

1 2 3 4 5 6 7 8 9 10

052918

Dedicated to Bruce, Mom, and Dad for
your loving support and prayers.
"For nothing will be impossible
with God" (Luke 1:37 CSB).

Contents

Introduction

It is not difficult to imagine what would happen if you loved a diabetic person who was not faithful in taking their insulin or whatever mediation they needed to eliminate the symptoms of their disease. The consequences would become very obvious in the way they acted, and then there would be more visible signs, such as amputations of limbs and other undesirable results. Diabetes is just one of those problems that requires the best medicine and medical care available, along with compliance with treatment guidelines.

In the case of a person with bipolar disorder (BD), there is no less need for the best medicine and compliance in taking it. And when the medicine is not administered, anyone loving the person with BD must struggle with the consequences. If you love someone with BD, you know that. You know how difficult it is for a person who experiences the rush of excitement and energy, the creativity and activity of the up times, to take anything that diminishes those times or eliminates them. Their temptation to stop taking the medication when those times are no longer there is severe. You also know that the person with BD looks for any sign that they are better and uses that as an excuse to stop taking the medicine. You know all that, and you know how you have reacted to it and how destructive those reactions can be.

This book will hopefully help you turn all of that around. My dream for you is to learn some new ways of dealing with the person you love that will enhance their desire to comply with what the doctor has prescribed. And it is my goal that you would have some new and better ways to respond when compliance becomes a problem.

Hopefully you are aware that the person you love is not bad, but sick. They may do some bad things, but if their sickness is properly treated, they can make better choices that produce better results in all of life and especially in their relationships. I have seen these results while working in an inpatient psychiatric treatment center. It has been a few years and the medication is much better now, but even then, people would come in with no hope of ever getting better only to discover that it was not their soul or heart but the organ in their head that was the problem. Treated properly, they would be discharged as new people with brand-new lives of hope and with a drive to have meaningful relationships that were redemptive and nurturing.

I have often quoted Jeremiah in the 6th chapter where he addressed the religious big shots of his day, warning them to stop giving superficial answers to the deep wounds of the people. It still happens today. Don't listen to anyone who thinks medication or Christian counseling is detrimental. Don't listen to anyone who advises that prayer eliminates the need for psychiatry. It does not. Prayer is powerful, and we must never cease praying. But we must add to that all of the things that transform our lives. And we need to encourage that in others. We need to help them see that God has created brilliant minds that know how to treat a brain that has the defect of bipolar disorder. I believe this book will give you what you need to help the person you love listen to the right voices that lead to hope and healing.

—Stephen Arterburn

CHAPTER 1

Life with the Person Who Is Bipolar

Most days, Janet lived on pins and needles.

As we chatted in my office I noticed the stress in her face as she explained why: "Being around my son, Jack, filled my whole being with anxiety—that feeling of doom as if something bad was going to happen. I told him once that he was my 'wonder child' because I always wondered what he was going to say or do next. It would often be completely out of the norm, either funny or frightening."

That wondering about what might happen next looked different when Jack was six, sixteen, twenty-six. What was consistent, for Janet, was the anxiety of being out of control.

She said, "It was hard for me to wrap my mind around his bipolar thinking. I couldn't figure out the logic. As a teen, Jack would start and stop activities—but not because he wasn't successful. In fact, it was the things he would excel in that he suddenly would quit without warning. He was a great soccer player, and the last game he played was the state championship where his team won. Then he was done, refusing to play for his last two years of high school. It seemed Jack could flip from obsession with an activity to hating the very same thing he once loved."

They wanted to help Jack find peace and to discover the underlying cause of this hectic way of life. Seeking the help of the family doctor and then from a professional counselor, they were told of the diagnosis of bipolar disorder, which explained how Jack experienced life. The experience of parenting a child who was bipolar caused Janet to feel anxious and isolated. "Parenting a child with bipolar disorder can take everything you have and more. In my case, Jack was extremely cruel to us, in his words. He questioned our love and motives relentlessly."

She went on to say, "There were no parenting books that I could read that spoke to my experience raising a mentally ill child. Friends could not relate to my parenting experience. I felt very alone and anxious." Perhaps you can relate to Janet's experience.

I can.

My Experience with Bipolar

Janet's experience resonated with my own experience of an adult in our family who lived with bipolar disorder. Though I'm a professional clinical counselor who serves people just like Janet every day, her stories of life with Jack sounded a lot like scenes from our Thanksgiving dinner table and other family gatherings. The details were different, but the chaos was the same.

The hope I held on to in my own family, the hope I had for Janet, and the hope I have for you is that the person living with bipolar disorder is so much more than their diagnosis. As Janet described Jack, she didn't have to tell me that he was loved, gifted, talented, creative, athletic, and intelligent. Because Jack was created in God's image, I assumed it. Because I could recognize the unique strengths and giftings of my own family member, I assumed it. As we journey together, I will remind you that your loved one is not his or her diagnosis. She's not her behavior on her worst days. Your loved one is, like you, a unique, complicated, beautiful individual who is loved by God. My hope is that, in these pages, you will find insight into your loved one and yourself and, more specifically, that you will find a way to thrive that's not contingent on your loved one's behavior. Because I've seen what's possible, I have hope for you today.

Generations

Cynthia, another client of mine, describes her own family's difficult history. She knew what it was like to live with those who weren't well: "My maternal grandfather, mother, and one of my brothers all have bipolar disorder. Their refusal to seek help added a struggle and burden to their lives and for those of us in their wake."

Cynthia's mother, like her, had grown up in a home impacted by mental illness. She offers, "My mom told us about Grandpa's rage. Something would set him off, and he would beat his only son while the others witnessed the pain. He didn't trust anyone close to him and felt like the world was in ruin." Though the disease looked different for Cynthia's mother, the themes were the same. Cynthia said, "Mom would go from being a workaholic to barely getting out of bed. She went through extreme highs and lows, like when she came home after having back surgery and proceeded to clean the house and move living room furniture, including a large organ and piano, by herself. Stepping in to assist her led to acts of rage, screaming, and her storming off."

As a child, Cynthia didn't have access to the help and support that could have made a difference in the life of her family. "I honestly wish I could have been able to drop my mom off at a place of help, but unless she was suicidal or a risk of harming someone else, that was impossible. There needs to be more help for the families who suffer in silence."

I believe that there is hope and help for families like Cynthia's and a family like yours. My prayer has been that this book will give you the tools and insight you need to live well. Though you can't control the choices or behaviors of your loved one, you can begin making healthy choices that allow you to flourish.

James

James, a pastor, came to see me when he could no longer manage his relationship with his wife. He told me, "My wife isn't the person I married. I mean, she looks like her, and I know it is her, but her bipolar disorder has taken over." His was a story I'd heard many times from spouses, children, and parents. They, like James, discover that they are in a situation they did not choose. And, like James, they realize that their future might look different from the one they once imagined.

James began living a life he'd not anticipated when his wife was diagnosed with bipolar. She was in her early thirties, and they had two small children. James said, "I had to come to terms with a *new normal* when she was first diagnosed. We have been open with our congregation, which has allowed others to share their struggles. It doesn't make it easier. Coping with her moods and the many unfinished projects around our home is a part of my reality now. I am committed to her, whoever she is now, and have grieved the loss of the woman I married."

Although heartbreaking, the journey James describes is a peek into what many families that include a person with bipolar mental illness will experience. There may even be signposts for the journey ahead of you today. You will need to release your ideas of who you believed your loved one to be. You can share your experience with people you trust. You will grieve what you've lost. You'll release what you cannot control. And you'll keep loving the person in front of you. Though the way forward may not be what you imagined for your life, trust that there is a way forward in which you will experience well-being.

Walking with a Friend

Before I'd ever considered a career in mental health, before I had resources to make sense of my experience, I witnessed the toll that mental illness could take on those who loved a person who suffered with it.

When I was very young, my best friend, Mary, lived five houses away from me. We'd tromp back and forth between our backyards and bedrooms every day. Before I had words to describe it, I noticed that Mary's mom was different. She was the life of every party, even when there wasn't a party. I loved her playful attitude and thought she was the funniest mom ever.

When Mary's mom was depressed, though, it felt like that vibrant woman was completely absent. Where had she gone? I learned later that she had received electroconvulsive therapy (ECT) treatments. She was also overmedicated, which created more difficulty than the illness itself. She'd spend many hours staring out the front picture window of their home. When she was hospitalized, I didn't understand why she wasn't around.

Mary's mom was first diagnosed with bipolar disorder—or "manic-depressive illness," as it was known in the '60s—when we were in third grade. Throughout our childhood, she continued to be in and out of the hospital.

When I look back, I can remember the sadness and fear that perpetually showed in my friend's face as she lived through the ups and downs of her mother's condition. She was suffering, and I had no idea how to care for her.

Light-years before I ever thought about being a therapist, I had a front-row seat to the effects of a devastating illness. And I would see this illness take over many more of those I knew and loved as my life continued.

What It Means for You

Bipolar mental illness can be a terrible disorder. But that doesn't mean that there isn't hope. While a diagnosis can evoke fear and pain, it can also offer a rubric for understanding what can feel so very confusing. It provides an explanation for past behavior and can even point you toward a path forward.

And that's where this book comes in. Maintaining a relationship with an individual with bipolar disorder is complex and challenging at a variety of levels. The key to living well as you navigate a relationship with your loved one hinges on two things: understanding and love. The two are inextricable.

If you are open to learning about the disorder, if you're eager to understand why your loved one says the things she does or acts the way he does, you will be giving a gift to your loved one and to yourself. You won't be able to move forward into healthier living until you understand what your loved one is facing.

While valuable, understanding on its own won't do you much good. You could read every book ever written on bipolar disorder and still continue to suffer in relation to your loved one. The win, for you and for the person you care about, is for that understanding to move from your head to your heart. The information I'll share with you in these pages becomes useful and effectual as you live out love. As you discover some of the causes of bipolar disorder and understand how it affects your loved one, you'll be better equipped to *love well*.

Loving well when a loved one lives with bipolar disorder is twofold. You can learn strategies to love your child or parent or spouse or sibling better. Discovering what helps and what hurts will help you love the person with the diagnosis. But as you grow in your understanding, you'll also be equipped to love yourself well. And that's no small thing. When Jesus commands us to love God and love our neighbors the way we love ourselves, His assumption is that we already love ourselves! You are worth loving, worth protecting, worth respecting. Your love for the person who suffers must always be balanced with a healthy love for your own needs.

Eggshell Living

Marcus grew up in a home with a mother who had undiagnosed bipolar disorder.

He says, "As a child, I walked on eggshells every moment of every day. I read the room, I read the mood, I read the expression on my mom's face, on my dad's face, I read their voices, and I read the silence. I developed a sixth sense … reading 'emotional space.'"

This hyper-attentiveness, necessary for his emotional survival, caused Marcus to bend his behavior to the environment around him.

He reports, "I went through my childhood conforming to my mother's emotional space every single day. If she was stable, I could be a good kid and do my chores without rocking the boat. If she was depressed and hadn't come out of her room, then I'd better keep up with my chores *and* hers or my dad would end up blaming me for her rage when she would come out of that room and find things out of order."

And as those in relationship with BD have discovered, there's ultimately no way to do everything "right" enough to compensate for the person with BD. Marcus learned this the hard way.

"If she was manic," he says, "well, look out. The very act of doing my chores could bring out her paranoia, and I would find myself at the business end of fury, accused of doing my chores just to manipulate her into being nice that day. It was usually a 'nobody wins' sort of battle, one that sometimes concluded with attempted suicide or total disappearance, which then meant a stint in the psych ward." No matter what Marcus did or didn't do, his efforts weren't enough to do what his mother needed to do for herself.

And as he moved into adulthood, Marcus brought the old patterns of reacting to a person with BD with him.

He says, "My acquired sixth sense, built as I learned to navigate the ups and downs of my mother's disorder, essentially became the guiding compass of my adult relationships. If I could read someone's unreasonable emotional space, and conform my words, actions, and reactions in a way that made them comfortable ... then I felt complete. I had successfully accomplished the only job I knew how to do in a relationship!"

In a functional family, children learn to notice and meet their needs by imitating a healthy, loving adult who sees their needs and meets them. However, having grown up in a reactive environment, where his mother's needs eclipsed his own, Marcus had never learned to do that.

He explains, "By ignoring my own discomfort and needs—which I didn't even realize or acknowledge I had until my late thirties—and making sure the other person was settled and okay, I could tell myself that it had been a good day. But as I strove to meet the needs of everyone around me, I ended up ignoring my own—and I suffered greatly because of it."

Marcus's journey bears many typical marks of people in relationship with someone who has BD: he learned to be hyper-alert, he tried to improve the situation by over-performing, and he ignored his own needs. If your own relationship with someone with BD began in adulthood rather than childhood, it may look a little different, but I suspect you can relate to Marcus's situation.

Because a return to health requires the participation of the person with BD, you may or may not be able to "help" in all the ways you'd like to. What you can do is to take care of yourself. If you don't acknowledge and care for yourself—and for your children, if your spouse is bipolar—you will lose. You will lose every single time. You will lose out on developing healthy relationships with friends, family, and a significant other. If you keep yourself anchored to the roller coaster of bipolar disorder without caring for yourself, you will lose out on experiencing the joy of fully embracing your own life.

If you're ready to care for yourself and embrace your own life while maintaining a relationship with someone who has bipolar disorder, let's press forward.

Essentials

As you discover ideas in this book that help you walk in life-giving ways, you'll begin to recognize what will work best for you. A strategy that works for one family might not work in yours. But requisite for every journey are boundaries, self-care, letting go, and forgiveness. I want to give you a peek at what those have looked like in one woman's journey and encourage you to discover what these do and can look like for you.

Boundaries

Boundaries—invisible but real separations between you and others—delineate where you begin and end in a relationship. When your boundaries are weak, you can feel overwhelmed by the others around you as they exercise too much control in your life. In a relationship with someone with BD, you might be the boundary-crosser by doing for your loved one what they have the ability to do for themselves. Perhaps you take on the caregiver role when the person hasn't asked for your help. If you're feeling overwhelmed, you may need to pay attention to your boundaries. The best book on the subject is *Boundaries* by John Townsend and Henry Cloud.

Sally has a sister who lives with BD. Though Sally has been intentional about trying to maintain good boundaries, she no longer pretends that whatever situation has been caused by BD isn't happening. Sally says, "I notice the behavior, explain why I'm choosing to respond as I am—by hanging up or leaving or finding another way to care for myself—and then I follow through." Last Thanksgiving, Sally had to practice implementing those healthy boundaries. Now she knows a bit better how to navigate family holidays. She says, "If I walk in the door for a holiday dinner at the time we're supposed to eat and the turkey is still frozen in the sink, I deduce that we're likely in the midst of an episode. My boundary is that I'm not spending the next several hours 'fixing' the situation if my loved one is in no mental state to be around people." Years of experience have taught Sally that "fixing" rarely fixes! She details the response she practices today: "I make sure she's well enough to be alone or with whoever is there, and I explain I will gladly come back another day. This usually creates an outburst, but at least I have not walked out without an explanation, even if she doesn't comprehend it or remember it later."

Self-Care

Self-care means that you are aware of your own needs and that you find ways to meet them. It starts by knowing how you feel and what you need, and then it moves toward addressing those needs. This may seem like a simple concept; however, when you are focused on helping someone in a high-maintenance relationship, you begin to lose focus on your own self-care. It can be as simple as taking a minute to assess your condition: Am I tired? Hungry?

Thirsty? Lonely? Angry? These simple questions can be a starting place. Sometimes guilt interferes with our self-care, and we need to remind ourselves that there isn't anything wrong with needing something to eat when we are hungry. That sure sounds simple, yet in the throws of the chaos that can be part of this relationship, we often delay our needs to deal with others' needs.

The obvious next step is implementing a solution: if you are tired, rest—even if it is just a five-minute time-out for yourself, sit in a quiet place and close your eyes. If you are angry, take a walk outside. Thirsty? Drink some water. Do something to address your need. These examples are simple, and as you become more aware of your personal needs, you can create your own ways of meeting those needs that are just right for you. We cannot give what we do not possess, and self-care helps us as we are helping others. Caring for yourself can include many different things, but the biggest need will be time away from the crisis, and sometimes that is the most difficult need to fill. It can feel selfish, yet it can be invaluable to the relationship and definitely helpful for your ability to navigate the maze of the disorder.

After years of bending over backward to accommodate her loved one, Sally finally decided that she was worth caring for, too. Today, she's learned how to ensure that her own needs are met. Sally says, "It wasn't until my adult years that I realized I needed to reprogram the messages in my head. I had to reprioritize. Though my default had been, 'How can I make you comfortable?' I learned how to ask, 'What do I need right now?'" Making this switch can be difficult, but it is best for everyone. Sally describes this new way of living in this way: "Because my thought processes have been rewired to acknowledge what I want and what I need, I'm no longer constantly waiting to react to what is happening around me. It doesn't mean I'm not willing to be a good hostess or to accommodate someone else. It simply means that my own needs are now part of the equation." Sally's choice to function differently benefits her, and it benefits others. She says, "If I am healthy and whole, I can be stronger for others. I still 'read the room' no matter where I am, but I no longer take on the responsibility of becoming a doormat so someone else can feel better."

Letting Go

Letting go means that you are able to extricate yourself from an emotionally difficult situation—especially one in which you are so invested in finding the remedy! If you are experiencing tension, a feeling of constriction, this is a sign that you need to experience release. That's easy to say and harder to do, but with practice, you will recognize when you need to let go of the control you are mindlessly exerting. When you recognize this tension—maybe if you are in a conversation with your loved one and they are not hearing you—and you sense the frustration rising in you, take a step back instead of reacting. In fire emergencies, we teach children to stop, drop, and roll. You can practice something similar for letting go: Stop the struggle, Drop the issue, and Roll away from the tension. You don't have to settle every score, and there may come a better time to address the issue if it is truly something that needs to be settled. We often get entangled with emotional webs that are not life-and-death issues. Letting go is recognizing when your need to control is controlling you and choosing to release control.

Letting go isn't easy, and learning to do it well takes time. Sally says, "It took a long time for me to get to a place where I could let go of the past in order to move on to more productive ways of engaging with my bipolar sister. But eventually, I got back in touch with that little girl who used to hide under the kitchen table, waiting for a raging episode to pass, and I told that little girl, 'You are okay. You are safe.'" In order to let go, Sally needed to offer herself the kind of care that she really needed when she was a child. She says, "This set me free in the present to let go of blame and burden and to find more productive ways of engaging and managing."

Part of "letting go" for Sally was releasing her cares to God. One of the tools she used to do that was prayer. Sally says, "I always had complete faith that God would lead me if I let Him. In order to let go of my past wounds I experienced in relationship with my sister, I had to bring everything before God in prayer and faith and trust that He would provide a way forward." Graciously, God did.

Today, God is ready and able to receive the cares of your heart as you release them to Him.

Forgiveness

Forgiveness is like tearing up the "IOU" and releasing another from their debt. And you are the one who benefits! Forgiveness is often a big decision, especially when you have a reason not to forgive. However, forgiveness is for your benefit because it releases you from having to manage the debt of the offense. It isn't easy to forgive when someone has hurt you, but if you choose not to forgive, the wound gets bigger as time goes on, and you are the one left with the infection, pain, and heartache. Forgiveness isn't simple, but it is a choice that releases you. It isn't as easy as "forgive and forget." Rather, it's "I forgive because I won't be able to forget and move forward in my healing without first choosing to forgive." It isn't a free pass for someone to hurt you repeatedly, but as you forgive, recognize that people are imperfect and are capable of failure (as are you). Recognize that BD changes a person, and they are often hurtful because they themselves are in pain. It's not an excuse for them to act in whatever way they want, but it is recognizing that the disorder causes them to behave in ways they don't always have control over. Forgiveness is a great gift to yourself, allowing you to be free of the bitterness and resentment that unforgiveness plants in your heart.

Also, you may need to ask for forgiveness in order to experience release. Maybe you got angry with your loved one because of the frustration in the relationship and you are feeling guilty for being so angry. Maybe you sense resentment building toward them because of how BD has changed them and you are short tempered with them. We are all human and have faults. If you allow yourself to be vulnerable in asking for forgiveness, you are also showing them you are working toward a better relationship, despite the challenges of BD. Forgiveness is essential to a loving relationship and is beneficial for both.

At the end of the day, be gentle with yourself. Loving someone with bipolar disorder means you have lived through traumatic experiences. And it means that there will be challenges in your future. Even at varying degrees of distress, bipolar disorder will span an entire lifetime. Don't expect the roller coaster to stop. It won't, not really, not for them. But be grateful that you have the choice to buy a ticket for the ride or decide to sit it out.

Sally says, "When my sister is properly medicated, I am able to recognize her sensitive spirit and her desire to be a good sister, friend, mom, wife. And I try to rejoice in the experiences that got us this far, to a good place 'right now.' It's not easy. The shadow of bipolar disorder is cold and dark. But it's part of who I am, and I will rejoice in the journey the Lord has given me."

Beginning the Journey

Martha's son was diagnosed with bipolar disorder when he was fifteen. Like many families, there was a season of chaos and confusion prior to diagnosis, and there was—and forever will be—"life after diagnosis." Without minimizing the challenges, I want to suggest that there is power in understanding. Learning about the disorder is like placing new tools in your tool belt that can help you and help your loved one.

Martha understands what it's like to witness distressing behaviors without understanding them and also knows how empowering it can feel to move forward after a diagnosis. Martha explains, "Before I knew what was going on with my son, I felt hopeless. Watching your child, who has been blessed with so many gifts, struggle so hard, and not knowing what was wrong or how to help him is a hopeless feeling." Though life wasn't all sunshine and rainbows when her family received a diagnosis for her son, it did mark a shift in how they were able to face and deal with the illness.

Martha says, "When the doctor suggested that Richard had Bipolar II, I wasn't really surprised. Although I wouldn't have guessed it, when I learned more about it, I looked at our family history and read everything I could about bipolar, and it really made sense."

It finally *made sense*.

"I feel guilty," Martha confesses, "that I didn't recognize what was going on with him earlier. If I had, perhaps he wouldn't have missed out on opportunities to get help."

Naming what was really going on was an opportunity to get help and move forward. It was for Martha, and it can be for you, too.

Don't give up hope. Life with a loved one who lives with bipolar illness can still be one of joy and fullness—especially as you learn to navigate this difficult path with tools and help from others. As you continue the journey of understanding and loving your loved one who has bipolar disorder, remember the words of the psalmist: "I waited patiently for the LORD to help me, and he turned to me and heard my cry. He lifted me out of the pit of despair, out of the mud and the mire. He set my feet on solid ground and steadied me as I walked along" (Psalm 40:1–2).

To move forward with your loved one, it will help you to know and understand their story. Understanding the disorder, having empathy for the sufferer, will bless them and bless you. In the next chapter, I'm going to give you some ways to understand what your loved one is experiencing. My hope is that you will experience peace in the chaos and will have a greater confidence in knowing you are not alone. As you read on, know that I know your story is uniquely yours; however, you will gain insight from others' journeys, and you will be encouraged as you realize others have found their way through the challenges.

CHAPTER 2

What You're All Experiencing

One of the most encouraging phrases in a struggle is when someone says to you, "Me, too." We need to know that this isn't just my issue or my problem; it is encouraging to know someone else has walked this way.

Bob was a well-loved and respected member of his small town. He worked hard to provide for his family and was a volunteer as well. He was an encouragement to many people in his life, and anyone who knew him felt like they were special to him. But his life started spiraling out of control with risky behavior, adultery, and ignoring the responsibilities to his work and family. The choices he made did not resemble the man whom everyone knew and loved. His wife was devastated when he lost his job and reputation.

When the loss of his job and his out-of-control behavior, including his infidelity, made the newspaper in the small town, his wife was overwhelmed with the pain of exposure. She mused to herself, "If he had had a heart attack or had died, there would be sympathy and understanding, but instead there is gossip and judgment." He was eventually hospitalized for suicidal thoughts and risk, and then attempted to follow up with ongoing therapy and medication. His struggles continued because he wasn't complying with treatment and doubted that he needed help, and his life unraveled. The family relocated in an effort to start a new life. But it didn't take long for Bob to begin experiencing the same struggles and taking risks, which ultimately caused the end of their marriage. His wife had endured enough pain and had done more than her share of supporting him in hopes he would continue in treatment. The defeat she experienced because he was not able to comply with treatment was like losing a huge battle she had been waging.

When Bob, who was diagnosed with BD, looks back on his experience, he says, "I've ruined so many people's lives. I'm still so depressed and so full of shame that I can hardly face myself in a mirror daily. I had the whole world in the palm of my hand, and now I can't apologize enough for the shame and pain I brought upon my family."

He lost his career, his family, and his reputation as BD took over his life. His "new normal" has an underlying fear that all can be lost, and the pressure is great to keep the normal going. The family, in the wake of the disorder, is also recovering, finding their own new normal. After his marriage ended, Bob's ex-wife had to support their family, working while feeling the greatest grief of her life. The family economics changed dramatically. Each of Bob's children began adjusting to the loss of a father who was still alive, just not present in their daily lives.

Today, twenty years later, Bob's children have developed their own new relationships with their dad, remembering the good times and feeling the sadness of the loss of what could have been while creating new connections as they are able. Each one knows how precious the time they have with their dad is because they know it can be taken away so quickly.

Life Interrupted

Mental health issues interrupt our plans for a happy life. They unravel whatever "normal" we had hoped for. The first disruption that bipolar disorder creates in a person's life can seem like a one-time occurrence—until it becomes a series of episodes. And with each episode, the relationship changes for both the person with BD and those closest to them.

Even as we have more clarity about bipolar disorder, as far as diagnosis is concerned, the impact on our loved ones and our families is fraught with emotion. It's not as easy as marking boxes on a checklist. However, the problem of mental illness, specifically BD, has a larger impact than just the immediate family and loved ones of the person who has BD.

The challenges of treating people who are diagnosed with BD are multi-layered. The disorder is in constant fluctuation for some folks, chronic with acute episodes, which is just the nature of the disorder. The symptoms can typically appear initially in adolescence or early adulthood, but they can go undiagnosed for years due to the lack of consistency and severity in symptoms. Some folks experience their first manic or depressive episode but do not seek treatment. It isn't usually diagnosed until it begins to be a problem and the person can see a pattern or until they experience a crisis moment or event.

What Is Bipolar Disorder?

Diagnosis is the first step to understanding what is happening, and it can provide a framework for better understanding your loved one in what can be a very difficult season.

The Diagnostic and Statistical Manual of Mental Disorders (DSM-5), published by the American Psychiatric Association, lists criteria for diagnosing bipolar and related disorders. This manual is used by mental health providers to diagnose mental conditions and by insurance companies to reimburse for treatment. It has information to help identify mental illnesses but does not offer treatment plans or processes.

There are many descriptions that fall under the bipolar disorder category. Some describe what has happened in the past and others detail what the patient is currently experiencing. Have you watched as your loved one's mood changes without cause? Perhaps you have seen them get super focused on something like music or art, and it causes them to stop everything else as they work on it, driven by the inspiration. Sometimes you see them in a passive state, eventually just not as interested in life as they normally would be. To get a handle on all this, let's look at how BD is described in the professional manual.

Bipolar I disorder means the person has experienced one manic episode, which might have followed or have been followed by a depressive episode. When the person experiences mania, it may require hospitalization, and it may also trigger a break from reality called psychosis. Mania is hyper energy combined with rapid thought processes and activities. If your loved one has had a manic episode, you know exactly what this looks like. Some manic episodes can be dangerous and severe.

Bipolar II disorder means the person has had a depressive episode, one that is at least two weeks long, and at least one hippomanic (elevated mood but not full mania) episode that lasted at least four days but not a manic episode. This isn't a milder form of BD. It is a separate diagnosis. The depressive periods with this form of BD can cause significant impairment for the person.

Cyclothymic disorder describes a condition in which a person experiences many periods of hypomania symptoms and depressive symptoms, typically more mild, for a period of at least two years (one year for children and teens). Symptoms occur at least half of the time, and do not stop for more than two months in that period.

There are other types of BD that are related to other medical conditions as well as those that are induced by use of substances and medication.

Is It Really Bipolar Disorder?

The biggest challenge with diagnosing BD is the multitude and variety of symptoms that can fit into the category. As you reviewed the descriptions, you may have thought, *Yep, they have this, and that and this, too* … That's not unusual! Knowing the types of BD disorders can be enlightening and informative as well as scary and depressing. It can feel like you are walking in a maze: one minute, you are sure of where the exit is—only to run right into a wall! The diagnosis is helpful and can give direction, but you and your loved one may be walking around in that maze for a long time.

Some of the symptoms listed you will recognize in yourself because we all experience one or two of these on some scale but not to the intensity that your loved one with BD is experiencing them. And to complicate it further, they experience times where they feel "normal," and yet some fear when the next episode will begin.

A person needs to have at least three or more of the following symptoms during a specific period of time, exhibiting noticeable changes from their usual behavior. The Mayo Clinic identifies the symptoms that mark a manic or hypomanic episode:

- Inflated self-esteem or grandiosity
- Decreased need for sleep
- Unusual talkativeness
- Racing thoughts
- Distractibility
- Increased goal-directed activity (either socially, at work or school, or sexually) or agitation
- Doing things that are unusual and that have a high potential for painful consequences—examples include unrestrained buying sprees, sexual indiscretions, or foolish business investments[1]

Different Episodes, Same Disorder

What is the difference between manic and hypomanic episodes? You probably have recognized a manic episode in your loved one: they have an elevated mood and high energy, they become focused on an idea or issue, and they will be driven to complete the task. It may cause them to miss work or school. They sometimes will withdraw from social activities or relationships. And there are times that they may experience a break from reality known as psychosis, which may require hospitalization. And none of this is a result of drugs or alcohol or medication.

The prefix *hypo* indicates *lower* or *less than*, and so the hypomanic episodes are a noticeable change in their mood and activities; it just doesn't get to the extreme where they miss work or school. They may be energized, but it won't cause them to stay up all night to finish the project they were focused on. The idea is that you notice an "unevenness" to their mood. One friend described it like never knowing what would walk through the door—"having to take their temperature."

The depressive episodes of BD have symptoms like depressed mood and loss of interest in many things that the person normally would be interested in. They may be sleeping all day or not sleeping at all, which then causes fatigue and low energy daily. They will experience either weight loss or weight gain, and in children, they will have difficulty gaining weight. They will have low self-worth, obsessive thoughts on guilt—real or imagined—and will focus on things that may or may not be true. This causes an inability to concentrate, indecisiveness, and thoughts of death, suicide, or planning suicide. You will see an obvious change in their mood and functioning, including loss of interest or pleasure. Sometimes they will tell you: other times you will notice it or hear from other people who are in relationship with your loved one. The symptoms would have to be serious enough to create disruption (missing work, school, disconnect from relationships) and aren't the result of something else like grief, alcohol, or drug use. If you observe these in your loved one, ask them if they think they might be experiencing depression.

Big Picture

About 4 percent of the adult population in the United States will experience bipolar disorder. It is more common in women, and the average age of onset is twenty-five. Men have an earlier age of onset. Hospitalization is greater for those who have BD than any other behavioral health care diagnosis, and the management and health care costs for treatment of bipolar disorder are in the billions of dollars in the U.S. Many patients who are treated for BD are also frequently treated for other issues, both psychiatric as well as other medical conditions. BD has been said to be the most expensive of all the behavioral health care diagnoses—more than twice as much as depression per individual because of associated loss of work and absenteeism. Early intervention and treatment can help decrease these costs.[2]

More than 75 percent of patients take their medication *less* than 75 percent of the time.[3] That means that if your loved one is not taking their medication, you and they are not alone!

While these statistics may be surprising to someone who is not affected by bipolar disorder, it is not a surprise to those who are. It is not a disorder limited to the United States. Bipolar disorder statistics from the World Health Organization (WHO) indicate bipolar disorder is the sixth leading cause of disability in the world.[4] There are many who struggle with this disorder, and the value of research and treatment has made a difference, but there is more work to do.

The medications that are most common in the treatment of BD are mood stabilizers. However, the process of finding what medication works for each individual is often a challenge for the patient and the caregiver. There is no perfect recipe for medical treatment because each medication serves a different function and the response from each individual is also unique. Being a caregiver or just in relationship with someone going through this process can create frustration, fatigue, and anxiety of your own. It is a process that is necessary to the treatment of BD, and finding a good combination or singular medication takes time.

There are people who are diagnosed with BD who also experience anxiety disorders and chemical dependency issues. Some general health issues—like obesity, diabetes, cardiovascular problems, and migraines—are some of the issues that occur with BD.

Much research is being conducted throughout the scientific community to understand bipolar disorder and how to treat it successfully. A recent study found crucial opportunities to manage bipolar disorder early are being lost because individuals are waiting an average of almost six years after the onset of the condition before diagnosis and treatment.[5] Many mental health professionals can also have difficulty distinguishing between a depressive episode and a phase of bipolar disorder.

Other Signs and Symptoms

There are other signs and symptoms along with the episodes mentioned above that can help you have more understanding of the different types of BD. Anxiety, feeling tense, feeling like they are not able to control themselves, and trouble with concentration due to worry can be experienced in BD. Feeling down even when good things are happening, also known as melancholia, is often part of BD. Sometimes there will be an odd reaction, like experiencing a positive mood in the midst of a depressive episode, which can be confusing. Some people experience a catatonic state—showing no expression to anything happening around them, almost as if they are frozen and separate from reality.

Peripartum onset, bipolar disorder symptoms that occur during pregnancy or in the four weeks after delivery, is also part of a BD diagnosis. If your loved one begins to have these types of symptoms mentioned above, it may be dismissed as "hormones due to pregnancy," but it can be helpful to talk with your loved one and seek help. Postpartum blues is common; however, there have been many women who suffer with BD, thinking it will pass as the baby gets older and the hormones settle down. Providing support and insight during this important transition in life can be invaluable for the mother and the child. If you are experiencing this with your loved one, check in with them—not to diagnose them on the spot but to offer support and help.

Seasonal pattern—moods or behaviors that change with the seasons, a lifetime pattern of manic, hypomanic, or major depressive episodes—is indicated in a BD diagnosis. Sometimes the change in the amount of sunshine has a major impact on the mood of a person. Some people need more light while others are affected by too much light.

You will hear the term "rapid cycling" with regard to BD. This means having four or more mood swing episodes within a single year. There may be full or partial remission of the symptoms in between the different types of episodes. If there are four episodes of depression, then perhaps it's followed by a hypomanic episode, which would describe an example of rapid cycling. Some people diagnosed with BD only have experienced one episode (of depression, mania, or hypomania), and this would not be rapid cycling. It isn't a description of how "fast" the symptoms occur, rather the frequency in a given year or period of time.

Sometimes the symptoms for BD in children and teens are missed because of the normal ups and downs that are part of growing up and adolescence. If you notice that your child or teen may fit into any of these descriptions, please call your family doctor or see a counselor. If it isn't BD, nothing is lost; however, if it is, treatment can begin and may make all the difference in their life.

Even the diagnosing criteria are overwhelming! But it can also be affirming in what you may be experiencing as you interact with your loved one. Some clarity is gained as we discover we are not the only ones who have ever experienced the challenges of a relationship affected by BD. The person who has been diagnosed is not the exception, the odd man out, or without hope for help.

Relationship Challenges

Challenges to those who are in relationship with someone diagnosed with BD are as varied as the diagnostic checklists, from challenges with privacy laws, legal issues, safety concerns, as well as the anxiety of when or if there will be a crisis again.

As Janice, the mother of a son with BP, explains, "This is definitely a condition where the afflicted needs a 'wingman' to monitor mood, actions, medication, doctor appointments, and so on. I am thankful my son is compliant, taking his medication, going to the doctor willingly."

Janice, though, also faces a lot of challenges. She says, "I am frustrated that this condition and all mental health conditions have so many stigmas, and this stigma is one reason why it took me so long to convince him to get help. It's why he can't fully explain the gaps in his résumé, his exhaustion to people during a job interview, professors, or his acquaintances. I am frustrated that the medical care for this condition as well as other mental health issues is so difficult to find and to fund [many places do not take insurance], and that many times, they fail to look at the *whole* person. I am frustrated that, as a mom, I do not know how best to help my son."

Janice's frustrations also have given way to confusion, guilt, anger, and sadness. She says, "I don't know when I am being too firm, unkind, and unsympathetic as well as when I am being too soft and enabling him. I feel guilty that I did not recognize what was going on with him earlier in his life. Perhaps he wouldn't have missed out on opportunities if I had been more aware of what was going on with him and pushed a little harder for him to get help. I am furious that he has to carry this cross. He is an amazing young man with such a horrible affliction, particularly when he is depressed. I feel sad to watch him suffer and how he struggles with relationships because of BD. At times, I feel hopeless, and then I feel angry that I feel hopeless!"

It's not just the person with the diagnosis of BD who has a problem. Some of the challenges you may experience are emotional distress such as guilt, grief, and worry—it can feel as though you are being consumed by worry and stress. It can interfere with your own work, responsibilities, and other relationships. And then you feel guilty for being stressed because they can't help having a mental illness.

You experience disruption in regular routines, often having your plans changed due to an unexpected situation or phone call that they need your help or attending appointments for treatment. You may have to deal with bizarre or reckless behavior—there are times when the effects of BD create unexpected drama and consequences. You can't always walk away from choices made as a result of BD.

There will be financial stresses as a result of reduced income, health care costs, or spending sprees.

The strained marital or family relationships that can create changes in family roles—such as when a parent requires your care for BD or as siblings experience the effects of the disorder in their family—make it difficult to maintain relationships outside the family due to the awkward feeling that you can't be fully known or present. It is like the family secret, thinking that no one can know about the struggle that is going on in our lives.

You may experience health problems as a result of the stress of caretaking in a challenging relationship. Understanding the impact on you is just as important as you wade through the diagnostics with your loved one! You may get so focused on their problem and not pay attention to your own health and well-being.

Whether the illness is BD or cancer, there will be relational challenges as you navigate through your journey together. As you read through the list of diagnostic material and qualifiers and statistics and ... well, you may begin to feel like you will not get the clear and succinct answer you are looking for as you help your loved one. Your experience is uniquely yours, and my hope is for you to be better equipped for your own story as you read these accounts.

Connecting the Puzzle Pieces

Whenever we are in a relationship with someone who has a diagnosable illness, it is tempting to try to work the whole puzzle at once. If you have ever worked a jigsaw puzzle, you know one of the first steps is to turn all of the pieces right side up. If you don't take the time to turn them over, you will work in vain to put the puzzle together. This simple step takes time but is necessary. There are those who will then work all of the edge pieces together, and others will focus on one part of the picture in the puzzle. There isn't a "right" way to put a puzzle together, but it does require using all the pieces in the correct way for the picture to come into view.

Understanding even a small piece of this puzzle will help you in your relationship. As you turn over all the different criteria in the diagnosis, does it fit? As you work through the edges of the qualifiers, is the picture coming into view? Sometimes, there are parts of the disorder that you can piece together quickly, like recognizing major depressive episodes because they are staying in bed for days on end. The puzzle of a correct diagnosis and treatment can take time and cooperation from your loved one. You may become so focused on finding all of the pieces that you forget they have to be part of the process of putting the puzzle together.

Bipolar disorder is part of your relationship, but it doesn't have to be the whole relationship. You can be very helpful in the diagnostic part as you share with your loved one what you experience as you are in relationship with them. You can also be an extra set of ears if allowed to participate with the treatment process by going to the doctor's appointments to understand what the treatment plan is.

Preparing for the Journey

When flying, you are given the same speech about the oxygen mask, no matter what plane you may be aboard. The passenger should always fit his or her own mask before helping children, the disabled, or persons requiring assistance. That's easier said than done when the crisis hits! But just like in an emergency situation on a plane, life with a person who has BD requires the caregiver and loved ones to take care of themselves with as much diligence as they give their loved one. The person with the diagnosis becomes the focus, but the person in relationship will require support, information, and self-care. Sometimes, it will require putting on your oxygen mask—taking a breather and seeking your own support before offering assistance. The very things you would want your loved one who has BD to do are often difficult for you to do for yourself (support groups, rest, health care, exercise).

We can also experience a faith crisis—where is God in all of this? When you are overwhelmed with what is happening, remember "God is our refuge and strength, always ready to help in times of trouble" (Psalm 46:1). Even with help and support, there will be days, weeks, and years when you will wonder how you will get through this. It is true that there may be periods when you are so overwhelmed by their illness that you do not feel God's presence.

It is difficult to pray and easy not to study Scripture. However, the more we can build our faith and relationship with God in between the crises, the more ready we are to find our way to Him during the storms. Many times when we experience our lowest point, we experience God in a powerful way. Recognize that God is with you in this journey even when you may feel alone. During some of the most difficult times in our relationships, we can sense God in the stillness. "Be strong and courageous. Do not be afraid; do not be discouraged, for the LORD your God will be with you wherever you go" (Joshua 1:9 NIV).

Every diagnosis for BD is unique within the parameters listed in this chapter. Your loved one's experience and diagnostic criteria for their BD is their very own. And the same goes for your response to what they are experiencing—it's unique. You will have reactions and responses to what they are going through that will be different from what someone else does. When you are looking at resources for how to deal with the challenges, know that one person's plan might not work for your situation; but maybe a piece of what they offer will help you.

Diagnosis is a guideline to helping your loved one with the struggle they are experiencing. It isn't who they are; it is what they are dealing with. To reduce someone's identity to a diagnosis removes their personhood from them. They are more than their diagnosis. You are more than their caregiver, and your relationship, although it may be painful and confusing as well as loving and caring at times, is a precious part of your history and future.

It can feel painful to receive the diagnosis of BD, or it can feel like a road map has just been given to you for this journey you have been on. You have to learn to accept the diagnosis and also accept how your loved one wants to proceed with treatment. As you continue to learn about the diagnosis and their response to treatment, hold on to hope: know that there will be challenges and victories along the way. There are so many pieces and parts to understanding this disorder as you go through this journey with your loved one. You are not alone, and if you feel you are alone in this, take the time today and reach out to someone for support. It might be the very best thing you do for yourself.

CHAPTER 3

Embracing Empathy for Your Loved One

When you have a loved one who has been diagnosed with BD, you may feel some relief, finally knowing there is a definition for what has been happening and that you can begin to look for solutions. Yet bipolar disorder has many different origins, and its treatment is as unique as the people diagnosed. You who are in relationship with them have to face the struggle, but you have to do it from the outside. It is frustrating and scary, as well as a myriad of many other things that can move us from our foundation. While there are questions during the discovery of the disorder, there are many more questions that follow the path of treatment.

Remember the way Bob's wife said, "If he had had a heart attack or had died, there would be sympathy and understanding, but instead, with the BD diagnosis, there is gossip and judgment"? So many struggle with understanding what their loved one experiences with BD, how to offer support to them, and how to find support for themselves.

When you learn about the causes and origins of BD, you can embrace empathy for your loved one. Empathizing with their struggle instead of resisting their reality can be a great support and connection for the relationship. It can also help you find what you need for support for yourself.

There is a puzzle to work in every case of bipolar disorder, and each puzzle piece will help complete the picture, or at least give a better idea of what is in the picture. As we are able to see the person instead of just the disorder, we can begin to offer help as needed and also recognize where we have limitations—the edges to the puzzle.

Seeking Understanding

Diane said, "I wish the phrase 'mental illness' would be dropped and that people would use the correct term of 'brain illness.'" She knows that the brain is an organ like the liver, kidneys, and heart, and she has had many professionals explain how brain chemistry malfunctions. When the pancreas malfunctions, it causes diabetes. So when people hear "mental illness," they think all that is needed is to stop negative thinking and you will be fine—as if that were possible.

When Diane's son was diagnosed, it was a result of head trauma. He almost simultaneously experienced severe agitation and outbursts of anger, which were totally uncharacteristic of him. He would have difficulty sleeping, which triggered seizures and made it very difficult to find the right medicine for treatment. She helped him as much as possible, empathizing with the pain he was experiencing yet feeling at a loss as to what could help him.

Diane was frustrated as she watched her son change as a result of BD due to head trauma. He was not able to find relief and succumbed to the disorder through suicide. "I feel like I'm vent-ing, but the loss of my son drives my voice to help others in this situation." Her empathy has now begun to focus on helping other caregivers and loved ones of people with BD know someone else understands their struggle.

Searching for the Answer

Where did this come from? Is bipolar disorder inherited? Environmental? Personality or choice? Whenever we are faced with a challenge, we begin looking for answers in many different places. And the answer is yes, all of the above—except choice. No one chooses to have bipolar disorder. This isn't a lack of self-discipline, a failure to attain maturity, or the result of not making a decision to "feel normal" in their daily life. It is a brain disorder that is affecting their daily life! There are many contributing factors, and each person will have their own map leading to their diagnosis and treatment.

Reading about the different facets of the disorder can help you understand that each person experiences BD differently—but with similarities. You may need to keep notes as you recognize differ-ent components you see in your loved one. You are being a great support just because you are reading about what their struggle is! Understanding BD can be difficult, but you are being loving as you seek to know more about this disorder that is impacting your loved one and your relationship with them.

Bipolar disorder often seems to run in families, and there appears to be a genetic part to this mood disorder. There is also growing evidence that environment and lifestyle issues have an effect on the disorder's severity. Stressful life events—or alcohol or drug abuse—can make bipolar disorder more difficult to treat. Experts believe bipolar disorder is partly caused by an underlying problem with specific brain circuits and the balance of brain chemicals called neurotransmitters.[1]

While you are looking for "The Answer," you will find there are many factors contributing to quite a few answers. It isn't a simple math problem. The different parts of bipolar disorder in each person and their response/reaction to treatment constitute what will work or not work for them. The answer can become elusive and frustrating. What is helpful is accepting that it won't be *one* single cause or answer, but that each step toward a better life experience is part of the solution.

Sojourners

Bipolar disorder has been diagnosed in famous people and not-so-famous people. Financial status, political persuasion, and other socioeconomic factors do not play a part in who has BD. Sometimes that can be comforting when you feel like your loved one is the only one this is happening to. We can also learn from others' stories and experiences, perhaps uncovering something that would help us help our loved one. These people have, after all, traveled this road that you are on.

I remember years ago reading a list of famous people with the BD diagnosis and finding it to be encouraging and hopeful. As I read about the contributions to society from the people on the list, it gave me hope for those I loved and those I worked with who were struggling with the disorder. The stories below are just a sample of so many who, despite BD, have enriched the lives of those around them. The written histories of these people give insight into what we now recognize as BD even when they took place prior to the official diagnosis of BD. Through their life stories and the challenges they experienced, we continue to learn that BD is not a new disorder. And despite their challenges, they made a positive impact on the world.

Winston Churchill's family had a history of mental illness. His father displayed psychotic episodes during his life, and his daughter Diana would ultimately die of a suicide in 1963. Churchill himself called his own depression his "black dog."

His friend Lord Beaverbrook described what sounds like a bipolar sufferer when he said that Churchill was either "at the top of the wheel of confidence or at the bottom of an intense depression." Churchill's depression has been credited with his early belief that Hitler had sinister intentions when others did not want a confrontation. Possibly only a man who had experienced such lows could see no hope in someone else.[2]

Churchill's experience sounds like so many of the stories from family and friends of people with BD. His contribution to the world is undeniable, yet he was afflicted with a struggle that many are familiar with.

Jane Pauley, former anchor of the *Today* show and *CBS Sunday Morning* host, described in her biography about being diagnosed in midlife. She had been prescribed an antidepressant for depressive symptoms she had been experiencing. Her doctor asked if she had made any big decisions recently. "Dropping my head and my voice, I said, 'Well, I bought a house.'" She describes how the medication had uncovered an unknown risk for bipolar depression. "That it took five months to provoke the mood swings also known as manic depression was pretty surprising. And four months on steroids before that!"[3] Jane was fifty-one when she had her diagnosis.

Popular actress and singer Demi Lovato learned she had bipolar disorder after treatment in rehab. In 2010, Lovato entered rehab after dealing with depression, an eating disorder, and self-harm. She discussed her diagnosis in a 2011 interview with *People* magazine. "I never found out until I went into treatment that I was bipolar," she told the magazine. During the interview, Lovato said she had battled depression from a young age. Recently, the popular songstress talked to HuffPost Live about living with bipolar depression. "I was dealing with bipolar depression and didn't know what was wrong with me. Little did I know, there was a chemical imbalance in my brain," she says. "Because I didn't tell people what I need, I ended up self-medicating and coping with very unhealthy behaviors." After therapy and treatment, Lovato says she's in a good place. "Now I live well with bipolar disorder," Lovato says. "Happiness is a choice. Life is a roller coaster. You can make the highs as amazing as possible, and you can control how low the lows go."[4]

There have been many historical figures who have been suspected to have BD before it was possible to obtain a formal diagnosis. For example, Ludwig van Beethoven was known for his brilliant gift for composing amazing music that contrasted to his difficult life at home. Beethoven not only suffered from deafness, but he is also believed to have had bipolar disorder. Beethoven became deaf at an early age. He also suffered intermittently during his life with bouts of serious fever and headaches. Sadly, as he got older, the disease began to affect him more and more. He often pondered suicide, a common symptom of bipolar disorder. He also went through a pessimistic emotional period that had a negative impact on the output of his compositions. There was degradation in his manners as well as his personal appearance, which is a symptom of depression (caused by bipolar disorder), and that caused him to have rough relationships because of his unstable arguments and delusions.[5]

Actress Carrie Fisher, who recently passed away and who was known for her *Star Wars* role as "Princess Leia" as well as her activism for mental illness awareness, commented, "One of the things that baffles me (and there are quite a few) is how there can be so much lingering stigma with regards to mental illness, specifically bipolar disorder. In my opinion, living with manic depression takes a tremendous amount of balls. ... At times, being bipolar can be an all-consuming challenge, requiring a lot of stamina and even more courage, so if you're living with this illness and functioning at all, it's something to be proud of, not ashamed of."[6]

History of the Diagnosis

Bipolar disorder symptoms have been observed for centuries, but it took a few centuries for it to be given a formal definition and become an accepted diagnosis. A professional classification system for mental disorders, which was important to better understand and treat conditions, has its earliest roots in the early 1950s.

The term *bipolar* means "two poles," which describes the polar opposites of mania and depression. The term first appeared in the American Psychiatric Association's Diagnostic and Statistical Manual of Mental Disorders (DSM-3) in 1980. It was that revision that did away with the term *mania* to avoid calling patients "maniacs."[7]

The ancient Greeks and Romans, who used the terms *mania* and *melancholia* to describe what we now know as manic and depressive, also discovered relief in using lithium salts in baths. Lithium is now a commonly used treatment for bipolar disorder.

Unfortunately, historical treatment hasn't been treatment at all for people who suffered with mental illness. With limited understanding about how to help as well as about what these folks were experiencing, treatment was often a random guess at what might help. Worse yet, religious beliefs thought these people were possessed and should be put to death. Some of those erroneous religious beliefs still continue, and they further complicate the treatment process. Many people are confused, thinking, *All you have to do is pray more and God will heal you* or *You must not be dealing with sin in your life or you would be healed.* Thankfully, treatment options have continued to improve and are multifaceted in their approach.

The study of bipolar disorder has had many twists and turns, which is similar to the disorder itself. In the seventeenth century, the treatment for depression included music and dance. Centuries passed, and little new was discovered about bipolar disorder until French psychiatrist Jean-Pierre Falret published an article in 1851 describing what he called *la folie circulaire*, which translates to "circular insanity." The article details people switching through severe depression and manic excitement, and it is considered to be the first documented diagnosis of bipolar disorder. In addition to making the first diagnosis, Falret also noted the genetic connection in bipolar disorder, something medical professionals still believe to this day.[8]

Thankfully, research continues on the understanding and treatment of bipolar disorder despite the challenging differences in the disorder. Each of you who are helping someone with BD are also conducting your own research as you work to find relief for the disorder. Research is discovering what is happening, what helps, and what doesn't help.

Case Studies

Case studies that are part of the research tell the whole story of how BD affects the sufferers and the effect on their lives. You may recognize similarities in your loved one as you read these case studies, and it may help you understand what they are experiencing, and you may learn about different treatment options as well. These cases represent the range of people who experience BD. It isn't limited to gender, age, or socioeconomic factors. Case studies also help further the effects of treatment and research for the future.

A female, age twenty-nine, married, a mother of a two-year-old, had a history of depression, which could be disabling at times, and headaches. When she sought help for this current episode, she was severely depressed and had difficulty moving, suffered loss of appetite, had crying spells much of the day, and felt suicidal. At the time, she was taking Prozac, and she described herself as getting "manicky" on the medicine. She would be "rushing around, laughing a lot and having more anxiety." Her depression was worsening despite the Prozac treatment. She had previously tried Wellbutrin, but it caused sweating and fatigue.

There was a past history of concussion at age eighteen, when she suffered loss of consciousness. She also described a history of mood swings for many years, as well as a history of alcohol abuse when she was a teenager. The diagnosis of major depressive disorder didn't seem to fit after a poor response to the medication for depression. Prozac was discontinued because it appeared to be worsening her mood swings.

Family history revealed severe mood swings in both her father and paternal grandmother. Her grandmother would at times take to bed for long spells, and she had been hospitalized for "unknown reasons" that the family refused to talk about. She recalled that the secrecy was because of something "shameful" about her grandmother's condition and behavior.

With the new diagnosis of bipolar disorder, by including personal and family history, she was placed on 100 mg of Seroquel at bedtime. Within one week's time, she began to improve, including clearer thinking, more productive work being done, less depression, and more energy. Within five weeks of taking Seroquel, she was feeling "terrific." The young mother continued with support through therapy and felt more confidence and a feeling of control over her life.[9] Her whole life experience was dramatically improved through treatment and support. And because of her treatment, the family stigma has been confronted and changed.

A twenty-nine-year-old male, married, a carpenter, during a recent manic episode "disappeared" for three days, he engaged in unprotected sex with a stranger and used illicit drugs, including ecstasy and cocaine, and also exhausted the couple's joint bank account by spending money on drugs, alcohol, and gambling.

After he experienced the "crash" or depressive phase of his bipolar, his self-care deteriorated, and he experienced extreme feelings of guilt and shame. He suffered from ruminating thoughts about the ramifications of his manic behavior and felt extremely guilty and shameful about cheating on his wife and his drug use. He is anxious about the results of a blood test to check for sexually transmitted disease and is worried about his future.

This was his fourth admission to a psychiatric facility but his first in four years. His wife called for help because of his disappearance, and then when he returned, he was making suicidal statements such as, "I don't want to be around anymore" and "You would be better off without me." He has been defensive and secretive about his actions during his absence from home.

When his history was taken, it was discovered he had stopped taking his medicine two months before this episode. He said his medicine made him feel "bland" and that he wanted to see how he would do without medication. He had been stable on this medication for four years. He was anxious and depressed but had difficulty sleeping and low energy.

He described his childhood as "normal" up until age eighteen, when he noticed significant mood swings and periods of insomnia. Up until this point, he had a supportive peer group and was active in sports. He was first diagnosed with bipolar disorder at age nineteen and was prescribed lithium, which left him feeling weak and lethargic. He also suffered from loss of appetite and itchy skin. He regularly stopped taking his medication during his early to mid-twenties as he missed the euphoria associated with his manic episodes. He had to be hospitalized after each of these manic episodes due to the following depressive phase. He has twice attempted suicide. His first attempt, at age twenty-three, was a lithium overdose. He tried again at age twenty-four. Both times, a family member found him.

He believes that when his wife finds out about the extent of his excesses while "high," she will leave him. He feels he is a failure in that he had been managing quite well up until he decided to cease his medication. He cannot see himself returning to his business due to his perceived loss of reputation. His main concern relates to his wife's potential reaction to her discovery of the full extent of his behavior during his manic phase. It is difficult for him to think of anything past this. He has very little in the way of expectations at present. He does not currently see a future for himself.[10] This is not the happy ending he hoped for, but so many families experience this with their loved one. Reading about his internal struggle may help you have empathy for your loved one who may be dealing with similar thoughts. If your loved one has a similar story, find a way to offer hope to them. It could be a short conversation or just a word of encouragement that we will get through this.

Seeking Support

How can you help someone else in a struggle that you do not have but that affects you as if you do have it? You are an eyewitness to their struggle and to their decisions, and you feel at a loss as to how to empathize with them. Understanding the disorder, continuing to connect with your loved one, and letting them share with you what they experience is being empathic and can be very supportive.

A mom recalls her son's senior year in college. Before the BD diagnosis, she was not able to convince her son to seek treatment. He was struggling with depressive and manic episodes, which included anxiety. When he finally saw a campus counselor, he reported it was not helpful. He decided to go on a senior trip with his friends, and instead of an "I arrived safely" phone call, she received a terrifying call from him saying he was unable to leave the car.

Miles away, as he sobbed and described his anxiety to her over the phone, she felt helpless being so far away from him. She was able to talk him through that episode. He was finally able to check into his hotel, and he then stayed in the room for the remainder of the trip. He wasn't the only one experiencing anxiety, and the mom's empathy was helpful as he reached out to her in his struggle.

Loved ones of those diagnosed with BD describe their own experience of dealing with bipolar disorder in the relationship. Usually, they are the first to be affected, noticing the changes in their loved one, feeling anxious, fearful, angry, sad, and confused—as well as feeling the sting of the judgment and rejection from others. We all want the best for our loved ones, and when an invisible illness takes over, one that doesn't have physical evidence like a rash or requires surgery, it can be challenging to offer empathy. We are dealing with our own feelings and can be frustrated as to what to do and who can help.

Frustration is understandable—this disorder is confusing, and many times, you are left with the fallout of what they have done. Anger surfaces, but telling someone with a mental illness to snap out of it is like telling a person who is deaf to listen harder. Empathy doesn't mean lack of boundaries, free rein to do whatever feels right at the moment, or dismissing your own feelings. When you feel overwhelmed, you can ask for help—your empathy for them doesn't dismiss your own feelings. If you feel like you aren't able to offer empathy, it's okay—seek your support and discover what you need. Self-care will increase your ability to empathize.

We All Have Something

Regardless of the origin of the disorder or the type of treatment required, each person needs to be "seen" as a child of God. We deal with illnesses here on earth that were not part of the original plan. The brokenness of this world is part of our experience here, and we all need to help each other out.

A popular quote says, "Be kind, for everyone you meet is fighting a hard battle." The complete quote speaks to the strength of the battle. "This man beside us also has a hard fight with an unfavoring world, with strong temptations, with doubts and fears, with wounds of the past that have skinned over but that smart when they are touched. It is a fact, however surprising. And when this occurs to us, we are moved to deal kindly with him, to bid him be of good cheer, to let him understand that we are also fighting a battle; we are bound not to irritate him nor press hardly upon him nor help his lower self."[11]

This holds true for the person fighting the bipolar disorder battle as well as the caregiver. With so many variables on the causes and origin of bipolar disorder, learn to listen without judgment, ask how they are doing, and offer support where you are able. And finding support for you as you travel this journey will strengthen your ability to show empathy for your loved one. Your support system will need people who can listen to you without judgment, ask how you are doing, and offer support where they are able.

Brené Brown, an author and researcher, says this regarding empathy: in order for us to connect with the other person, we have to connect with something inside ourselves that knows that same feeling.[12] How difficult is this when we don't know what we feel or understand what they are feeling? Relationships, regardless of this diagnosis, can teach us more about ourselves, and empathy is one way we learn. When you are trying to share empathy and are unable to connect with a similar or same feeling as the other, it can be helpful to say, "I don't know how that feels; tell me more." And you don't need to fix the feeling—just be witness to it.

Embracing empathy will help this relationship as well as other relationships you are in. It takes practice, awareness, and vulnerability to embrace empathy. Practice with other relationships you are in, perhaps with a close friend or spouse who doesn't have bipolar disorder. Strengthen your awareness of how you might be judging or resisting hearing what someone is sharing with you; recognize the feelings that are coming up in you. And know that in order to embrace empathy, it will require vulnerability—taking the risk to understand, hear, and know what the other is feeling and experiencing. It involves asking, "How are you?" and waiting for a genuine answer when you would prefer "fine" as the response.

Empathy may be difficult if you have been hurt in this relationship or if you have had to set a boundary where you do not interact with the person any longer. Take time to heal those places with those who are safe: a counselor or a close friend. Recognize that empathy can also be had toward that person without having to be in relationship with them in person or face-to-face. For those who have lost a loved one who had BD and are still experiencing pain from that relationship, this can be a very healing process.

Whether famous or unknown, every person who has bipolar disorder has had their own story of their experience of the disorder and treatment. And loved ones and caregivers also can tell you about the story and struggle. The most important thing is that both stories are heard and are not left to fight the battle alone.

The passage in the Bible about the paralyzed man (Mark 2) reveals the power of support. "Four men arrived carrying a paralyzed man on a mat. They couldn't bring him to Jesus because of the crowd, so they dug a hole through the roof above his head. Then they lowered the man on his mat, right down in front of Jesus" (verses 3–4). These friends recognized their friend's need and were willing to do whatever it took to find healing for him.

So many have done exactly that for their loved ones—brought them to Jesus. Through tearful and anguished prayers, doctor visits, and therapy sessions, trusting that something would make a difference. You are doing what you know to do and are willing to do whatever it takes to help.

CHAPTER 4

Finding Effective Treatment

Karen struggled with depression throughout her adolescence, but her mom thought it was just part of the teenage experience. When it continued into Karen's young adult years, her mom suggested Karen seek treatment. Maybe, she reasoned, some medicine would help. Karen agreed to therapy but wasn't open to taking medication.

"I don't need medicine. I just need to give myself some time, be stronger."

The mother-daughter relationship was frustrating and painful as Karen would rage over the smallest thing and accused her mom of not doing anything right. Karen continued to experience bouts with depression and then asked her doctor if there was anything she could take for it, recognizing it wasn't going away on its own. The antidepressant helped at first, relieving the depression, but then she became manic and had to be hospitalized. Karen's mom felt entirely helpless as she watched her daughter being taken, against her will, from their home to the hospital.

While Karen was hospitalized, a new diagnosis was given: bipolar disorder. That changed the treatment plan. The new plan would include a mood stabilizer. As she began a new course of treatment, one that was based on the correct diagnosis, mom and daughter began to experience a new relationship. They both had a new understanding of what Karen was dealing with and were committed to continuing the course of treatment, including counseling, group therapy, and staying open to any adjustments that would continue effective treatment. Understanding the correct diagnosis and what the treatment plan would be offered hope for the future. While continuing to adjust to the "new normal," they are experiencing a new level of intimacy in their relationship. They truly have a silver lining.

How do you know when treatment is necessary?

When do you take steps toward helping your loved one find help, especially when you are not being asked for help?

What Is the Next Right Step?

When the person with BD agrees to see a professional and a diagnosis is made, another journey, one to find effective treatment, begins. It isn't a one-size-fits-all, and it can be as frustrating for the person who is providing care as it is for the one diagnosed. It will require more appointments than imagined and, sometimes, more rabbit trails than intended! Keeping the focus on finding what works will help when it seems there is no help at all. Taking the next right step will require cooperating with the patient and understanding that the next step may feel like it is a backward one. But it is all part of the path toward healing.

The extremes of the disorder also present challenges to finding the correct diagnosis. In Karen's case, her depression was more significant, and so she was treated for depression. Her manic episode was extreme; therefore, hospitalization highlighted the need for a new diagnosis and treatment plan. The BD individual usually seeks treatment during a depressive episode rather than when in a manic phase. However, motivation can be low when the person is experiencing depression, and they may be resistant or unable to express the need for treatment. This can be frustrating for those who are seeing the person suffer, and as much as they attempt to help, it will feel futile.

The extremes in mania can create chaos in the lives of those who have the disorder as well as those in relationship with them. It does, though, make it more obvious that there is a problem to be addressed and treatment sought. When the less obvious mood swings are the type of BD your loved one is dealing with, you may have more difficulty in knowing or recognizing what to do next. Honest and open communication with your loved one can help with knowing when and how to seek treatment.

Course Correction

Andy loved baseball, and his high school years were full of team spirit! When he received a scholarship to college for baseball, he looked forward to four more years of the same camaraderie. Practices began, and he began to experience disinterest. He shrugged it off as not being under a good coach and not feeling connected to his team. He quit the team, lost his scholarship, and was faced with an unknown future. His parents were confused and saddened by his choice and unsure of what was happening with Andy. He became depressed, disinterested in school, and dropped out.

After a few unsuccessful job experiences, he recognized this depressed feeling was more than just not playing on a baseball team. He was losing interest in life. His parents encouraged him to talk with someone, and Andy complied. He was diagnosed with BD, and he began to understand what was underlying all of the struggles he had been experiencing. With the correct medication and commitment to treatment, he had regained hope in his future.

Though it took Andy a while to find the right path, with the support of his family, he was able to find health.

What Will Work?

Traditional treatment is a combination of medication and talk therapy, which, in a perfect world, works the first time around. Perhaps you have experienced the hopelessness that comes with "bad" help. The frustration and discouragement when your loved one doesn't receive the help they need are coupled with the panic and fear as you watch your loved one struggle. As your loved one is seeking help, it may be helpful to consider the "failed" avenues simply as options that they no longer need to consider.

With medications, good communication with the doctor is essential because the medicines can complicate the process as patients experience adverse reactions. Which medicines are effective and tolerable is one part of the whole, along with compliance to the prescription and complementary treatment, like counseling. Many times, the process of finding the right medicine or combination of medicines can feel like a mountain-climbing expedition! For those with BD, feeling worse during the trial-and-error process of finding help can create more distress. Sometimes self-medication becomes part of the equation; use of alcohol, marijuana, and other illegal substances further complicates the goal of finding a treatment plan that will be successful.

There are many things the person with BD can do that are beyond the traditional treatment methods. Increasing the amount of daily exercise and the amount of light, such as natural sunshine or light therapy, developing regular sleeping habits, and eating a balanced and healthy diet can all have an impact on their response to treatment. Knowing what works for them is part of the trial and error of finding treatment that will help them.

Medicinal Help

Bipolar disorder is treated with three main types of medication: mood stabilizers, antipsychotics, and antidepressants. Each type and combination of them is unique to each person to whom they are prescribed. As the patient is working with the doctor on the medication part of their treatment, communication and compliance is extremely important to finding the best treatment. This is probably the most frustrating as well as the most assuring part of the process of treatment because when it works, it feels like they have their life back, but when it doesn't, it feels hopeless. But medicine, when it works—meaning the individual is receiving both the correct type of medication and also the correct dosage—can be life changing for the person as well as those who are in relationship with them.

As you come alongside your loved one in this process, encourage them to talk about the frustration they may be feeling or the doubts that this medicine "will be *the* one." Encourage them to talk through any side effects they may be experiencing, and encourage them to be compliant with the prescription to really know if the medicine is right. And follow up with, "If it isn't right, we will keep looking."

Many times, people with BD think they don't need medicine, that the mood will pass and they will feel better. Others don't like the way the medicine makes them feel, so they refuse to take anything and suffer through life. It can be frustrating as you try to help them, and you may feel resentment, thinking, *If only they would take their medicine, everything would be better.* If your loved one is resistant to taking the medicine, rather than confronting them, encourage them to talk with their doctor about what they are experiencing and their resistance to taking the medicine. The person with BD is ultimately the one who will choose their course of treatment, which is good when the treatment is effective and frustrating and frightening when it is not.

There are many people who refuse any medical intervention, and they manage the disorder through other processes. It is a personal decision on the part of the patient. If your loved one has decided to go with this course, communicate with them your concerns and create an open dialogue so they will let you know if they need more help. Accepting their decision and communicating your acceptance along with the option that they can change their mind at any time are valuable. This disorder is so nuanced that at any moment, they could decide they need medical help.

We live in a culture where we believe if you take a pill it will fix everything. The truth is that just a pill rarely does fix anything! Even when you have an infection, antibiotics work, but you will also need to rest. If you've suffered an injury, you will need to clean the wound, and you also need to take the antibiotic as prescribed. If you've ever taken an antibiotic, you know that once you feel better, you're tempted to quit taking the medicine. Similarly, many with BD reason, "I feel better, and I don't like taking medicine, so I will quit."

In the medical treatment of BD, the medicine can be a life-saver, but finding the right dosage and type requires patience and open communication with the doctor as well those in relationship with the patient. Encourage your loved one to share with you and their doctor any changes they are tempted to make with their medicine, or if they feel worse, better, or the same. All communication about their medicine can be helpful as you offer your support.

There are side effects with many medications that create additional challenges in the patient's treatment. Some create health issues that were not present before, which can become a big barrier because other medications will be needed to manage secondary issues. Diabetes, heart conditions, and weight issues are just a few examples of some of the health issues that may occur. Some of these happen because of the predisposition of the person, but they are often side effects of the medication. These health conditions also have an impact in other areas like their ability to work. Encouraging the patient to be open about how they are feeling with the medication, if there are adjustments that need to be made, and their level of adherence to the prescription can make a big difference in the treatment process.

Some people with BD are also struggling with alcohol or other drug dependencies that either preceded the diagnosis or came along with it. The treatment of these will be simultaneous and can have compatible benefits. Some of the addiction treatment can help the person with processing the intrusive thoughts, boundary issues, and relationship challenges that come with BD. The treatment for BD can help with the cravings for the drug or alcohol as well as the anxiety the person experiences, which may contribute to their dependence on the substances. Using alcohol or recreational drugs will impact the effectiveness of any treatment for BD. It can also endanger the life of the person with BD if the substances are mixed with the medications they are taking for BD. Be sure to share any concerns with your loved one, encouraging them to speak with their doctor or therapist about the issue of addiction.

Safe Next Steps

Hospitalization for BD is a common occurrence, and it is often seen in the depressive cycle, when suicidal thoughts or threats to harm themselves may surface. This can happen because of a mood change or a change in medicine, or some circumstance may trigger them, causing them to begin to obsess over the harmful thoughts. The difficult experience itself can create more shame and a feeling of failure for the patient as well as for the caregiver. Hospitalization can feel scary, overwhelming, and hopeless, but it can be a life-saving step for the patient.

There is often resistance to going to the hospital. Many times as I would be counseling families of loved ones in this stage, there would be resistance to taking their loved one to the hospital or calling an ambulance. One woman remarked that she had taken her sister to the hospital when she was experiencing suicidal thoughts. After the woman with BD spent a week in the hospital, she moaned, "It was the worst week of her life." I reminded her that because of that "worst week," her sister was alive and able to complain about that experience.

Taking that step to call the hospital is scary, but the hospital staff are professionals who can determine if your loved one needs to stay or is stable enough to be released. You don't have to take on the whole process—just one step, which in the case of calling the hospital or ambulance may be the best decision you make in helping your loved one in this critical stage.

When should you call the hospital or 911? Sometimes it is obvious: suicide attempt, debilitating depression, inability to sleep for days, mania, or psychotic behavior are all obvious changes in behavior that can be dangerous for the person with BD. You can also ask your loved one if they feel like they need to go to the hospital. They often will resist initially, but they may accept the offer for help.

The hospital or inpatient treatment process can many times be a "restart" for people with BD. A hospital stay is usually shorter, perhaps a week or two at the most, depending on insurance and availability of beds at the hospital. An inpatient treatment center may have a longer stay, sometimes beginning with thirty days. This stay may include an assessment, the creation of a treatment plan, participation in daily group sessions, education, and medical management. There are also many programs that are based on Christianity and offer Bible studies and worship as part of their programs.

These interventions can often create crises of their own, and the caregiver can get drawn into a power struggle. When resistance is met with resistance, nothing will be accomplished. It becomes a standoff creating more tension. The balance needed is truth and grace—there is a problem and we need more help. This connection is so valuable in the ongoing treatment for BD.

Finding the balance of truth and grace will include conversations with your loved one about what you are seeing and your concerns while also asking them what they are experiencing. Balance may occur for a day, or you might experience it for months at a time. An example of truth would be understanding the diagnosis, medical intervention, and treatment plan. Grace is offering space to your loved one, a listening ear for them as well as self-care for you.

Not My Issue

Non-compliance to any of the above interventions may also occur. Many suffer from the side effects, ineffectiveness, or simply "feeling flat" when taking medication to manage BD symptoms.

"I lost my creativity," said one client who decided to forgo ongoing medical treatment for her BD. She talked with her doctor about how she was unable to work as an artist because she relied on her "manic" phase, when many of her inspirations were the strongest. Her depressive cycles were short lived and managed with her counselor. She wasn't taking the medicine as prescribed, which created more side effects, such as physical illness, nausea, and the inability to drive. There were times when her depression was so deep she felt what has been called "the dark night of the soul." She lost her business, her home, and faced health issues through the years. However, she has re-created her life, is now employed, and has a sense of fulfillment in her family and life.

One Size Doesn't Fit All

The approach to treatment is as varied as each individual. Since BD has different facets, it requires multiple responses with treatment. People who are diagnosed with BD, and their loved ones as well, are sometimes offended when "advice" is offered on treatment approaches. Both the client and the caregiver can feel the fatigue of yet another way to "fix" the problem. Generally, acquaintances who offer suggestions mean well and want to help by sharing what worked for them or someone they know. In these cases, you or your loved one can take what you need and leave the rest. Sometimes, you learn something you hadn't thought of before, and it can be very helpful. Determining what is negotiable (which doctor or counselor) and what is non-negotiable (following a treatment plan) can be so helpful as you and your loved one seek help for BD.

When you are the support person and you are suggesting different treatments and therapies to your loved one, it can create tension in the relationship that can become toxic for both of you. How do you create a collaborative effort when the resistance is strong? What can you offer when help is not being asked for yet you see the struggle? When will the "right" treatment fix the problem?

This is where your support system will help. The treatment for BD is ongoing, unlike a disease like cancer where there is a resolution, such as remission. Bipolar disorder requires ongoing management. Acceptance of this fact is crucial to the steps on this journey. We often begin to think that the next treatment strategy will take care of this and that we therefore won't have to worry about it ever again. Life will resume, and all will be well with the world. You don't have to like what you have to accept; just accept the reality of the diagnosis so the focus is on what will help today.

One husband shared the impact his wife's BD had on him.

"I am devastated by what has happened. Jill was and is the love of my life—how could she do this? The whole neighborhood is talking about her and the man next door."

Jill had not been diagnosed with bipolar disorder and was untreated. She had been struggling with a depressive cycle, sleeping for most days, then without warning, awake more hours than not. She began to work feverishly in their yard, redoing the landscaping on her own. When the new neighbor offered his help, she accepted and then eventually had an affair with him. Her shame overwhelmed her, and she sunk back to the depression. When she revealed her affair to her husband, they sought treatment. She was diagnosed with BD and took the first step into a journey of healing. She began with medication and talk therapy as a first step, and she had her husband alongside her. Jill's father had BD, and she understood the devastation BD can bring if it goes untreated. She was willing to do whatever it took to manage BD, and she valued her husband's support.

Safety Instructions

As we talked about earlier, the instructions offered by flight attendants are to put on your oxygen mask before assisting anyone else. It's easy to hear but tougher to follow in a desperate situation. How do you put on your own mask when your loved one is in a rage?

What does that even look like? How do you recover after dealing with the fallout of the most recent manic episode?

There are many who will offer a simple, quick-fix, permanent solution to a complicated, slow process, a process that requires attention throughout the lifespan of the person who has the diagnosis. Even those who have had their own experience with BD or their family members will tell you what worked or didn't work. Sort of like "labor and delivery" stories; every mother has one, and it is unique to her experience. They may tell you which doctor or therapist worked for their loved one, and it can be helpful as long as you know it may not work for your loved one. The challenge you will have is your limited control over treatment since it isn't you experiencing the labor. Understanding this will help in a way that no drug can. The focus has to shift from remedies to treatment. All of us are changing, growing, learning each day, and so the treatment will shift accordingly. The relationship you have with your loved one will require patience as well as persistence. Making the choice to participate in the treatment is yours, and your own support, as well as treatment, will be part of the whole.

There will be times as you try to find help when you will be exhausted, frustrated, and feel like you are *done* dealing with the drama and the challenges, especially if your loved one asks for help and then rejects your help and acts as though you are the enemy. You will be on the edge of tears, or they may even spill over as you watch your loved one struggle through another episode. It is hard. It is confusing. It is frightening.

What are you doing for your own care and mental well-being? While you are helping with nutrition, appointments, household responsibilities, emotional support, and a host of other supportive measures, how do you take care of you?

Good nutrition, exercise, and maintaining personal health and well-being are essential for the caregiver. Bipolar disorder can create havoc in the life of the person who has the diagnosis as well as the caregiver, but both are in need of support and a plan of wellness.

Exercise has been called a natural antidepressant since it's a helpful way to lower stress, build confidence, get good sleep, take care of your body, and even connect with other people (if you participate in exercise with others). Many therapists who work with patients with depression or anxiety recommend taking a walk outdoors every day, regardless of the weather or time of year, to stay in touch with nature, the seasons, and the elements around you.

The goal is to develop and modify as needed a plan of response to the diagnosis. To this date, there isn't a "cure" for bipolar disorder, and so the "cure" becomes the treatment or the plan of action. What is your plan of action? How will you respond to this "new normal"?

There will be a time of grieving the loss of what you had hoped would be your life. Grief work is an important part of the treatment, both for the diagnosed and the support person. When the diagnosis has been made, there has already been some recognition that things are not as they should be. Taking time to work through the feelings you have will allow some space to deal with the other issues.

Grief looks different for each person, and you might not even recognize that you are experiencing it. Grief can appear as anger, resentment, or resignation, as well as sadness and depression. What have you lost with the BD diagnosis of your loved one? Spend some time writing out some of those feelings. Allowing them to come up and out will create relief. Grieving is a process and a part of life. Even in situations where there isn't a death, we experience loss, and it is valuable to recognize the loss. Listening to your loved one's losses with this diagnosis can also be helpful for them, and it can allow you to have greater understanding of their journey.

Anxiety occurs when considering what treatment options to take, and anxiety will appear again when waiting for the treatment to work—and once again if the attempt fails. The person diagnosed is also managing anxiety concerning treatment. When we can share our experience of dealing with bipolar disorder, it becomes a pathway to peace. Upsizing empathy is essential, as is doing all we can to love this person as they are, as Christ would. The definition of empathy is the feeling that you understand and share another person's experiences and emotions: the ability to share someone else's feelings.[1] But keeping good boundaries so that you are not as affected by their behavior is just as biblical as love. We want to be responsive, not reactive, and that is where empathy can help.

Prayer for Healing

Last, but certainly not least, prayer is a crucial part of the treatment process. As you walk with your loved one with BD, you can be praying for answers, cures, and solutions. Prayer can also be part of your self-care. Seeking the Lord for comfort, strength, and wisdom is essential as you deal with the stress, confusion, and feeling of futility as you continue to search for help. At these times, it may be difficult to find the words or thoughts to pray; however, the prayers of David from the Psalms can be a great help.

Psalm 86 is one that can be helpful for you to pray. David describes many of the feelings you may have experienced in your journey. If you haven't the strength to pray, it can help to read this psalm aloud:

> Hear me, LORD, and answer me,
>> for I am poor and needy.
> Guard my life, for I am faithful to you;
>> save your servant who trusts in you.
> You are my God; have mercy on me, Lord,
>> for I call to you all day long.
> Bring joy to your servant, Lord,
>> for I put my trust in you.
>
> You, Lord, are forgiving and good,
>> abounding in love to all who call to you.
> Hear my prayer, LORD;
>> listen to my cry for mercy.
> When I am in distress, I call to you,
>> because you answer me.
>
> Among the gods there is none like you, Lord;
>> no deeds can compare with yours.
> All the nations you have made
>> will come and worship before you, Lord;
>> they will bring glory to your name.
> For you are great and do marvelous deeds;
>> you alone are God.

Teach me your way, LORD,
    that I may rely on your faithfulness;
give me an undivided heart,
    that I may fear your name.
I will praise you, Lord my God, with all my
        heart;
    I will glorify your name forever.
For great is your love toward me;
    you have delivered me from the depths,
    from the realm of the dead.

Arrogant foes are attacking me, O God;
    ruthless people are trying to kill me—
    they have no regard for you.
But you, Lord, are a compassionate and gracious
        God,
    slow to anger, abounding in love and
        faithfulness.
Turn to me and have mercy on me;
    show your strength in behalf of your
        servant;
save me, because I serve you
    just as my mother did.
Give me a sign of your goodness,
    that my enemies may see it and be put to
        shame,
    for you, LORD, have helped me and
        comforted me. (NIV)

When we pray, it isn't just for a healing to occur. Rather, it helps our hearts and minds settle on God's power and wisdom in our lives. Otherwise, we can become so focused on controlling the situation or the person that we become weary in the fight. Our trust in God has been affected because of what this disorder has done to us, both the person diagnosed and the support person.

Acceptance is part of the treatment process. Understanding that there will be things we cannot control, change, or fix will require prayer! You are not alone in this, and it will be imperative to continue to connect with others, both those who are experiencing a similar situation as well as those who are a great diversion. Taking a "recess" can be helpful in the journey. It allows for rest, which can help prepare you for the next mile.

CHAPTER 5

Loving Them, Loving You

In the movie *The Wizard of Oz*, Dorothy's dog, Toto, keeps getting into Almira Gulch's garden, and she threatens to take him to the sheriff to be destroyed. Dorothy is begging her aunt Em to do something to fix the crisis, and she responds to Ms. Gulch by saying, "Almira Gulch, just because you own half the county doesn't mean you have the power to run the rest of us. For twenty-three years, I've been dying to tell you what I thought of you. And now, well, being a Christian woman, I can't say it!"

Aunt Em's remark assumes that there is a "Christian" response to another's chaos.

When you are close to someone with BD, you may feel constantly on edge, not knowing what the next crisis will be. When that crisis erupts, your reaction may not be as controlled as Aunt Em! There will be times when you have held your tongue when you are exhausted, stressed, and afraid of what is happening to your loved one, and there are other times when you will say things that aren't exactly biblical. The utter chaos of the disease can disrupt your intention of loving and helping the person in your life who is struggling with a disorder that is overwhelming them.

There will even be days when your faith in Christ will be tested. You love the person with bipolar disorder and want to be helpful and supportive, but because of the reactive nature of the disorder, relationships can be strained to extremes. Some relationships do not survive.

So what is the "Christian" response when you are in relationship with someone who is affected by bipolar disorder?

The Love Chapter

The thirteenth chapter of Paul's first letter to the church in Corinth offers a pattern of love that is distinctly Christian.

> Love is patient and kind. Love is not jealous or boastful or proud or rude. It does not demand its own way. It is not irritable, and it keeps no record of being wronged. ... Love never gives up, never loses faith, is always hopeful, and endures through every circumstance. (1 Corinthians 13:4–5, 7)

This passage is often read at weddings, stitched on pillows, used as a warm sentiment on greeting cards, and offered as a way of life for Christians to follow.

Putting it into practice, though, isn't always easy.

There are dark days in dealing with bipolar disorder when it becomes difficult to love. Your patience and kindness may be strained because of the way the disorder changes your loved one. It's easy to love someone when they are kind and patient toward you, but it's another story when that person has attacked you out of their own misery. It hurts, and it is easy to react in defense, and after it happens a few times, you may want to throw your hands up and quit. Are you unloving because you feel like giving up? No, your feelings are a response to the relationship fatigue. Are you unloving when you establish a boundary? The answer is no; the most loving action may be a boundary you set in a relationship.

One afternoon in my office, Kate bravely revealed the pain of her marriage to Jim. She was weary and frustrated about his ongoing resistance to seeking help for BD. He took medicine that had been prescribed but never went back for follow-up appointments, which only made the issue worse. His depression eventually cost him his company, and his manic episodes triggered family crises where everyone else was the object of his rage.

Kate finally reached her limit. She explained, "I'm sorry, but I couldn't do it anymore. He was not willing to seek help, and my children were afraid of him. I know it's not what God wants for my children, but divorce was the only answer. I wish it could have been different."

Their marriage couldn't handle the weight of the disorder. That doesn't mean that Kate wasn't strong enough, didn't love enough, or wouldn't try hard enough to make the marriage work. Love can be lost under the stress of this wily disorder. Kate made the difficult decision to leave her marriage in hopes that her children would be spared as much of the crisis and pain as possible. She was motivated by her love for her children. Knowing when to draw that boundary will require you to have people who love you assist in seeing the best next step.

Sending Out an SOS!

In the midst of crisis, it is requisite that you have your own support system—family support, friends, a therapist of your own, and a small group—to help you navigate the confusion and hurt that can occur in your relationship. You must be able to ask for help. It isn't less "Christian" or less "loving" to ask for help or to set boundaries to protect yourself and ultimately the loved one who is battling this disorder.

Sometimes we think having more people involved in the personal business of our lives will only complicate matters. We may be having a difficult time understanding our situation ourselves, and we lack the energy we believe we'll need to deal with the opinions and attitudes of others. That work is more than we want to take on. After all, how could others begin to understand what we are experiencing? And even if they do understand, how can they help?

Whatever image you have in your mind of what a support system looks like, set that aside and think about who you call when crisis hits. When you are feeling afraid of what is happening with your loved one, is there someone you talk to? If someone came to mind, they are part of your support system. If you couldn't think of anyone, you have some work to do. Doing that work, engaging the help of those who can offer support, will make all the difference in the world.

Many of you reading this will bristle at the idea of a support group. Others may already know that it is crucial to get through difficult times. Support groups are an invaluable source for connection, information, and encouragement. But it can also be a challenge to find just the right one. If you have no inclination to find a support group, perhaps you start by finding refreshment at a Bible study or a book club. It's like putting your toe in the water. It might feel cold at first, but then as you warm up, it can become a refreshing place to recharge.

All of us need people in our lives. When one of those people has a challenge like BD, the disease can create an isolation that grows over time. I know that finding a support group may feel overwhelming, but perhaps this week, you could take the first step of looking for one in your area by asking a few local members of the clergy if they can point you toward local mental health resources for family members.

Some of your support can be professional. It can be very beneficial to work with a counselor or therapist of your own to process some of what you are experiencing in relation to your loved one with BD. It can be helpful to you to have someone who understands BD but is focused on helping *you* in your relationship. Therapy doesn't have to be every week, necessarily, but it might be weekly for a time. But if a crisis happens, you will have this support. Just knowing that help is available can bring relief.

Family and friends can also be a great part of your support system. Inviting them into your journey can help you feel less alone. At the same time, it's possible that they could be a challenge if they are driven to fix everything or to tell you what you or your loved one should be doing. Take the risk to share your concerns, frustrations, and fears with someone you have trusted in the past. Maybe the first conversation is short, but in time, you will have built an ally in your life. Someone you trust who can walk this road with you is quite a find!

No Quick-Fix Solutions

One wife I've worked with said, "My husband was recently diagnosed after me bugging him to get help for the last years. I'm glad he is getting help, but I am struggling with it. I feel like everything is falling on my shoulders." She added, "His medication is still a 'work in progress,' so while I understand that this all will take time, I am at the end of my rope. He seems worse now than before meds. I feel alone and sad all the time. I have so much anxiety. I know that, when I get upset, it actually makes things worse for him, but this is all so new to me."

Her experience isn't uncommon. The fallout of bipolar disorder in a relationship is what each person experiences as a result of the behavior associated with the illness. Sometimes, the distress might be what you feel in the aftermath of a fit of rage, resulting in fear and trauma from the attack. Other times, you have to cope with seemingly endless days of depression. This disease is not just happening to the diagnosed person. You're affected, too.

When we feel like we are being trampled over and disregarded, we don't feel loved. Creating boundaries for your own well-being and safety will create the best environment for love to flourish in the relationship. You don't love when you are not fully present in a relationship because you've checked out to keep the peace. Failing to create healthy boundaries isn't loving. Love requires presence, and sometimes that will mean you have boundaries that the other person wouldn't choose. He or she may even rail against them. But just because the other person is protesting doesn't mean the boundaries aren't healthy. Maintaining them is hard, but it can be the most loving thing to do.

A friend recently recalled how her son, diagnosed with BD, dealt with the rapid cycling type of the disorder.

She explained, "You never knew what the day would bring as he was growing up. There were often explosions of emotions in the house—both his and my reaction to his!"

As he became an adult, the chaos was taking over the family, and it was time for him to move out on his own. She was fearful that it would be too much for him, but she felt that if he stayed, she would not survive. He has been able to have stability as he manages his disorder while living a full life outside of the family home.

She says, "Our relationship is loving, supportive, and closer than ever."

Her son called her recently but didn't leave a message, and she immediately had a sense of panic rise up. When she called him right back and he didn't answer, the anxiety began to swell. She texted him and asked if everything was okay. He texted by saying he was just checking in and he was fine. Then he texted back, "Thanks mom for checking" with a heart emoji. She went on to say that their history gets stirred up at times like this, but then she realizes how far they have come and how he is doing his life well.

Her choice to establish healthy boundaries has allowed both of them to thrive and flourish.

Loving Well

The account of Jesus and the rich young ruler is an example of healthy boundaries. The man asks for eternal life, and Jesus responds with an answer that disappoints the man. Mark explained, "At this the man's face fell, and he went away sad" (Mark 10:22). Even though Jesus can see the man's reaction, Jesus doesn't run after him to change his mind, reword his answer, or give him another chance. And the preceding verse affirms that "Jesus felt genuine love for him" (Mark 10:21). Practicing boundaries is one way to show love because we create clarity in the relationship. It reveals who we are, who the other person is, and what the values in the relationship are. Without boundaries, there is confusion and chaos. The rich young ruler was holding on to his money, youth, and notoriety. Jesus recognized this and allowed the young man to make his choice. He didn't try to manage him; He just presented him with truth.

Think back on a time when you were in conflict with your loved one over a boundary issue. Perhaps he or she was not taking their medication as prescribed (a conversation that takes place many times with people with bipolar disorder). The boundary or request that they comply with the doctor's prescription for the medicine doesn't appear to be a huge request, yet it somehow develops into a crisis when it is not honored. Your fear of what will happen if they don't take the medicine combined with their resistance and rationale about why it will be fine creates conflict. In the midst of that whirlwind, your faith seems to get lost in the vortex. You begin to react in anger, demanding that the protocol be followed. To you, this doesn't seem like an unreasonable request. After all, you are trying to help them get relief.

In the wake of these struggles, you may feel the guilt and shame and the shoulda, coulda, wouldas. You may even experience negative self-talk about how they might do better if they had someone better equipped to handle their challenges. Maybe someone else, besides you, would be able to help them follow the treatment plan. You may even believe that if you were a stronger, better Christian—whatever that means—you would be "patient, kind, not irritable, or rude." It can become a cycle that destroys the relationship.

What does a Christian response look like?

When we are struggling, fear and insecurity can take over. We aren't sure of what will happen with our loved ones, or we are simply exhausted over the constant upheaval in our lives. We begin to seek control in the out-of-control situation and forget that in all of the chaos, God is present. Even though God is near, the circumstances steal the peace He promises.

A Christian response is just that: a *response,* not a reaction. Healthy responses are cultivated through our own self-care as we pay attention to the wounded places in our hearts. Just as your loved one has triggers as a result of the disorder, you do too! They are a natural result of your experience in this relationship as well as your own life experiences. Your relationship with Christ will help you in your own healing journey as you seek Him through prayer and study of the Scriptures, connecting with other believers and experiencing God's grace.

Your natural reactions are just evidence that there is healing needed. They signal that you need to learn new ways of behaving and responding. They are not a condemnation of your imperfection.

Sisterly Love?

One Bible study teacher—I'll call her Nancy—related her experience with her twin sister, who had bipolar disorder. The family had struggled with her sister's health care needs and the repeated resistance to offers of help. The sister ultimately became homeless and lived on the streets for years, creating more stress as the family wondered where she was and worried for her welfare. Despite countless attempts to bring her into her own home, find her employment or education, and help her with basic necessities, this sister would return to the streets. Why would she resist help and shelter? She wasn't home long enough for treatment to experience relief or stability, and she would impulsively leave the safety and care of her family.

When she would return to the family, they loved her by offering food, shelter, clothing, and a warm embrace back into the family. But her disordered mind would begin to create conflicts, focus on trivial issues, and make them into major conflicts, ultimately giving her reason to leave again. She had become addicted to drugs and alcohol while living on the streets, which complicated the challenges further. Love opened the door for her return but couldn't make her stay within the safety of the family.

Nancy prayed countless nights for her twin sister, not knowing where she was, worried for her safety and well-being. Nancy didn't think God was listening. If God was listening, He wasn't acting fast enough in answering her prayers. One day, a police officer appeared at her home to let her know her twin sister had been found dead near a dumpster in the city. Her worst fears had come true, and then the onslaught of regrets began. If only she had known the right answer to provide help, her sister would be alive. Perhaps if she had just done a little more for her sister, she could have been healed. What if she would have given her more attention as she struggled with the disorder? Ultimately, Nancy reached out to her loved ones who had been supportive throughout this journey and shared her grief and pain. They comforted her with assurances that she had done her very best to love her sister. Her own healing would now begin, and she would slowly begin releasing the struggle she had been carrying for many years.

Nancy loved enough to welcome her sister back home but knew she couldn't make her stay. Nancy felt hopeful and wanted healing for her sister, and her heart was broken when her sister left home. She gave shelter to the one who had walked away from the family, and she would endure being misunderstood and being accused of being stingy when her heart was generous toward her sister. Love allowed Nancy to release her sister, even though the risk was great, knowing her sister had free will to come and go as she wanted. Despite her loss and the complicated relationship, her love for her sister was the motivation.

Loving the Unlovable

What does it look like to love when the actions and behaviors of the person are unlovable? What does loving the person with BD look like? It may look like you are assisting with their treatment process. If they are resistant and combative, loving them may mean setting a boundary and letting them manage the care process on their own. Confusing as it may be, loving them might require letting them experience consequences instead of forcing your control in the situation.

Loving the person with BD will definitely include being available to listen to what they are experiencing, giving them time to share about what they need or want, what they are thinking about. It also includes honestly expressing when you need to conclude the conversation. Sometimes, your loved one may be obsessed on a topic and want to tell you every detail, and your most loving gesture would be to let them know you can talk for about ten minutes.

Loving the person with BD when they are in a depressive episode might be as basic as asking them if they are depressed. A simple question can offer a lot of support to a depressed person. You can follow up with, "How can I help?"

The biggest expression of love when dealing with BD is courage: not being afraid to ask the person what is wrong or if there is anything they need help with. It also requires courage to establish a boundary as an act of love. Saying no can feel very unloving but may be the most loving thing you can do, as many times people with BD can overwhelm the relationship.

One response that does interfere with loving the person with BD is to maintain that the disorder is a consequence of sin in the life of the person who has the disorder. This is not true. If this is your belief, it is imperative to work on transforming this false belief in order to have a loving relationship.

Losing Hope

Our hope can be diminished as we are challenged with the effects of the disorder on our loved one and our relationship with them. We can lose faith in God's ability to make a difference in the person or in the disorder. You may even doubt your own ability to manage the new normal and accept that the crisis will become a usual way of life.

How can we continue to trust God when we have asked Him to heal, change, and provide help and a million other things, and nothing seems to be changing! It may cause us to believe that God isn't listening, isn't able, and is so far from our need that we have to handle it on our own.

You may hear negative messages insisting that nothing will change this situation. It is essential for you to continue to hope for improvement in this situation. Notice I didn't say "cure." Improvement is the goal. What positive changes do you experience in your life as a result of this relationship? That sounds like a strange question, especially if you are reading this and have recently faced yet another blowup!

You also feel the pain that your loved one is going through. Not just the pain they may have directed toward you. Your heart breaks because of the struggle they experience. When they share with you their joys, you may become concerned it will go too far. When they talk about the depths of their pain, you may hope it won't overtake them. You are probably the one person they want to entrust with their journey. This is the reason you need support from others.

Hope Is Found

The psalmist offers wisdom for those in crisis, exhorting them with these words:

Hear my prayer, O LORD;
>   listen to my plea!
>   Answer me because you are faithful and
>   righteous.
> Don't put your servant on trial,
>   for no one is innocent before you.
> My enemy has chased me.
>   He has knocked me to the ground
>   and forces me to live in darkness like those
>   in the grave.
> I am losing all hope;
>   I am paralyzed with fear.
> I remember the days of old.
>   I ponder all your great works
>   and think about what you have done.
> I lift my hands to you in prayer.
>   I thirst for you as parched land thirsts for
>   rain. (Psalm 143:1–6)

This journey is harder than you expected and will require more than you think you are able to provide. When you are wondering how you can "fix" this, the "why" question starts in your mind, or the "if onlys" are mocking you, the best response is to ask for help. You may not necessarily ask for it from the person who has the disorder, although sometimes they need to hear from you, but you may ask for help from people who are not in the midst of the struggle.

Many Christians struggle with not hearing answers from God when they pray, and then when they are in the day-to-day struggle, they respond in anger, despair, resentfulness, and as a result, they feel guilty. When you are experiencing the stress of this relationship, recognize you need support. You cannot do this alone. And as you are waiting to hear from God, trust that He will provide people, resources, and insight into what the next right step will be. You aren't "doing it wrong" when you experience anger, despair, sadness, resentment, and a myriad of other emotions that will surface. It isn't because you haven't prayed enough or given enough or just can't figure it out.

The impact of mental illness on the loved ones of the diagnosed person has nothing to do with their relationship with God. However, the response from the loved one to the one diagnosed *will* be impacted by their relationship with God. Strengthening your relationship with God will help you, will equip you, and will be an essential part of your own self-care.

We don't want to think about the worst possible thing happening. For some, the worst thing has already happened, and the defeat is unbearable. The psalmist describes it perfectly: "LORD, you know the hopes of the helpless. Surely you will hear their cries and comfort them" (Psalm 10:17). The Lord knows your pain and will provide strength and comfort for you. It will come through as you seek support, prayer, and Scripture. It will come through as you allow yourself some time for recovery. Grieving is not optional; it is a necessary part of the healing process. Recognize your need for support, and actively pursue help.

Begin to trust those who are part of your support system. When you are carrying the load on your own, you will be tempted not to trust because disappointment will be part of the journey:

disappointment in your loved one, the medical support, the counseling support, and God. It will feel as though no one completely understands and therefore cannot be trusted. You will disconnect, initially because it feels better than trying to trust and explain what your reality is. Then you might choose to stay disconnected because to risk again is seemingly far more painful than just being isolated.

Your faith in Christ is manifested in relationships. The Lord provides encouragement and strength through others. When you have to set a boundary with your loved one, it helps to have your support team to provide biblical wisdom, encouragement, and clarity. When you are attempting to provide everything for your loved one and they are resentful, combative, or resistant, your support team will help you accept the limitations.

Praying for Peace

Only God is God. You will not be able to provide all that your loved one needs, understand all that they are going through, or have the solution for them. Prayer is an essential part of our support system. The Trinity is the perfect small group! When you are in the midst of a crisis, a common response is to pray. Commit to making prayer part of your daily life, not only as a plea to God to fix everything, although those may be the majority of your prayers for a while! Daily prayer will equip you to face whatever the day brings: joy or sorrow.

The Serenity Prayer has been a vital part of daily reflections for many people for many years. You may be familiar with the first part of the prayer, and you may even have it hanging on a wall somewhere in your home. The complete prayer is a full picture of enduring peace. Sometimes, we don't know what to pray, and this can be a place to start.

> God, give me grace to accept with serenity
> The things that cannot be changed,
> Courage to change the things
> which should be changed,
> and the Wisdom to distinguish
> the one from the other.
>
> Living one day at a time,
> Enjoying one moment at a time,
> Accepting hardship as a pathway to peace,
> Taking, as Jesus did,
> This sinful world as it is,
> Not as I would have it,
> Trusting that You will make all things right,
> If I surrender to Your will,
> So that I may be reasonably happy in this life,
> And supremely happy with You forever in the next.
> Amen.[1]

CHAPTER 6

Try This

Have you ever wanted a handbook with simple step-by-step instructions to deal with the different situations that occur in a relationship with a person with BD? I have never been an expert at following instructions. I seem always to discover leftover screws when I am assembling preassembled furniture! The good news about this book is that it isn't exactly step by step, but it does offer an overall view of what you can expect. Unfortunately, there isn't one specific set of instructions to each individual situation; however, there are a few recurring themes that seem to present themselves regularly in these relationships.

In my practice, as well as my personal relationships, it was helpful to have some direction in these scenarios or at least one next step to address the issue. Even if it isn't the exact situation you are dealing with, there may be something that will help you in your relationship. It can also be helpful to discuss with your loved one what you are seeing or experiencing with them, not to be critical or even micromanaging them. Perhaps you mention, "I want to really understand what you are going through and share what I see, not to be critical, but to offer insight as we work through the details, finding the best treatment." This can build connection as you seek a treatment process together.

When a Diagnosis Is Rejected

What about when the initial diagnosis has been given, yet your loved one is not quite convinced that it is an accurate diagnosis? They recognize there is a problem, and they begin to explain to you that they don't need your help or the doctor either, for that matter. A struggle begins; you are frustrated and attempt to talk with them about how you are just trying to help. They may shut down and refuse to talk with you or begin to be angry or even begin to rage. You may feel some fear, anger, and possibly want to rage back at them. The conversation stops, and you are left without resolution.

What can be helpful for both you and the person with BD is reflective listening. When you're able to reflect back what a person has experienced or expressed, he or she feels seen, heard, and known.

For example, if they say something like, "There is nothing wrong! *You* go to the doctor since you are so convinced something is wrong!" When this situation happens, try to allow some space and time between their reaction and your response. Your response might be something along the lines of "This is pretty upsetting to you, isn't it?" This response, an example of reflective listening, is a way for your loved one to know you are not fighting against them; instead, you are trying to let them know you hear their frustration. Obviously, tone matters. Try to communicate that you are really *for* them.

Usually, when reflective listening is suggested to any client, the first response is resistance because you want a resolution, not further discussion! However, in those moments where there is high resistance and lots of drama, the first step is to let them know you hear their concerns. You aren't agreeing or disagreeing, just listening, which is very powerful to someone who is struggling with BD. It is also helpful to you because you do not get lured into a power struggle and debate about what needs to be done.

Your goal in using reflective listening is to have them agree with your statement of observation. When you see them nod or say, "Yes, this is upsetting," you have communicated that you are listening—that you hear what they are expressing. If they disagree or express that you don't "get it," you can follow up with a statement like, "I am sorry, tell me what I am missing." This will allow for some clarification, and it also sends them the message you are staying with them, that you want to stay engaged in understanding what they are communicating. Reflective listening is a great communication technique for any situation where you want the other person to know you are listening.

You might be thinking that this will not resolve the issue of going to the doctor or confronting the reality of the diagnosis. The emotional volatility is overwhelming in that moment! Resolution is a moving target: in this situation, the resolution will be that they are calmer and have experienced your support through listening. It will allow opportunity for finding a solution as emotions subside. It will create trust that you want to help them and want to find resources to help with the problem.

When you encounter resistance on any issue, remember to create space and allow some time to respond to the issue instead of reacting to the emotion and resistance. When you meet their resistance with your own resistance, a bigger problem is created. You don't want a standoff with them, one where you are determined to make them see things your way. Reflect back to them what they are focused on until they agree that you have heard them. If they have calmed down enough to your point of view, you can share. But it may have to wait for another time. There won't be a quick resolution to any confrontation; however, this will provide a long-term approach to addressing issues and finding solutions.

When a Sufferer Remains in Bed

What do you do when your loved one is experiencing the depression part of bipolar disorder and remains in bed the majority of time? How can you help when they aren't able to function at their job or school or connect with family or friends? You may experience some anxiety as you wait for them to get moving again, you may fear their losing their job, and you may grieve as you watch the days pass with no improvement. You can feel powerless in their depression, and the anxiety builds as you are aware they are in bed for the majority of the day. The days of the depressive cycle feel like they are never going to end, yet the hope of each day is "Will this be a better day?" Depression that goes untreated gets worse, and this is where you may have to be more direct with helping them get treatment.

You might consider having a conversation when they are up and out of bed about going to see the doctor or therapist. Perhaps you could try saying to them, "It seems like you are really down. Do you think you might be depressed?" They will probably agree, or they might say they are just really tired and equate the fatigue to their medicine or not feeling well. You can ask them if there is something you can do to help, perhaps offering to make the appointment for the doctor or therapist. Keep the suggestions and problem solving to a minimum since depression creates a brain fog, and they can feel overwhelmed with the choices. You might say, "I can make an appointment with the doctor or counselor and will be able to go with you. It will help you feel some relief." You can also offer to go with them to the appointment to provide support.

If they don't live with you, this can be challenging. You may begin to feel the anxiety creep in when they don't answer phone calls, texts, or even the door if you go visit. Ask them to check in with you: it can be a quick phone call or text to let you know that they are feeling depressed, not up to a visit, but are safe. I once heard that depression is the brain requiring "deep rest," aka "depressed." When the depression cycle hits a person with BD, it usually follows a manic phase, which would make sense. Understanding this can help you as you reach out to them in this cycle.

Their depression also has the potential to be contagious—not literally, of course, but you can experience depression as you deal with their depression. The low mood and activity can drain you as you attempt to encourage and lift them up. You will need to seek help for yourself from a friend, counselor, or doctor to address any depressive feelings you may be having. It can help you just to share what you are experiencing even if there isn't a solution presented.

The opposite of the depressive cycle is the mania that occurs with bipolar disorder. What do you do when their manic mood creates havoc for you and for them? Sometimes, the highly elevated mood isn't destructive, but they may be awake for hours, and you still need to go to work or at least get a good night's rest. This is where your boundaries will be tested, and it's best you have a plan in mind before this occurs.

One of the first things to do is to recognize this when it occurs and identify it with your loved one. You might say what you are seeing: "Wow! You have had a burst of energy, haven't you?" The tone of this question is said in a more lighthearted way, a non-defensive stance, just identifying what you are experiencing. The goal is to bring attention to what might be behavior or a mood that could escalate to a crisis level.

The elevated mood can feel good even to you, especially after a depressive cycle. Seeing your loved one in a good mood, happy and feeling inspired, bringing with it a burst of creativity and productivity can bring a sense of relief to you. The elevated mood isn't a problem until it is a problem. Sometimes with the manic cycle, there will be sleeplessness—for days on end. Initially, it can feel inspired to the person experiencing the burst of energy; however, you and they will begin to feel the effects of lack of rest, and the anxiety will begin to build around how to calm the energy down so that rest is possible. Communicating your concerns, asking them if they see there is a problem with not sleeping, and presenting some options can be helpful. With BD, the challenge is the dramatic mood swings and their effects, and the goal is to have less of the dramatic mood swing, without flatlining the person's moods.

If there is a specific behavior or activity that is occurring because of the manic mood—for example, shopping beyond their ability to afford or perhaps outrageous and impulsive purchases—there are some steps to take. However, it is usually after the fact that you are aware of such purchases. If it is a spouse or someone you have combined your finances with, you will need to have boundaries on credit card accounts or savings. This is a much bigger conversation than just identifying what you are seeing. You will have to take action, set boundaries, to do what you can to prevent more damage.

Natural boundaries occur with spending—money runs out. However, credit cards and buying on credit can delay the boundary, and your loved one may end up in debt beyond what they can repay. You might feel like you have to step in and pay, or they may guilt you into repaying the debt, saying things like "I bought it for you, for us!" If you find yourself in this situation, seek the help of a credit counselor, and they will help you create a plan to get out and stay out of debt.

When a Loved One Threatens Suicide

What do you do if/when your loved one threatens suicide? How should you respond when they express to you they don't want to live anymore and want out of their pain and the pain they are causing everyone else? Many people feel afraid, and rightly so, when they hear a loved one express they want to end their life. It can create fear and anxiety in you, and you may feel like you are on pins and needles, holding your breath, wondering what to do to prevent this from happening.

Take the threat seriously, and ask them if they have a plan. This may be a difficult step for you, and it may feel like you are overreacting, but it is necessary. If they say they have a plan, ask them if they feel pressure to act on the plan. Again, it may be too difficult for you to have this conversation, and if that is the case, ask for help from someone—a professional or a trusted family friend. You can also call 911. This may also seem like you are panicking; however, it is better to call than to hesitate. A threat of suicide is serious and should not be ignored.

Recently, someone asked me about a family situation concerning suicidal ideation and was hesitating because, years before, a family member was suicidal and they had called 911. The relative was hospitalized for a week and described it as the worst experience in their life. However, they have the ability to complain about that now, years later, because they are alive. Suicide is a permanent decision to a temporary feeling.

When I was visiting someone in a psychiatric hospital, after they were focused on suicide, they shared with me a phrase that puts this into perspective: "I am having a suicidal thought, and I feel _____." Suicidal is not a feeling; it's an action. When someone says they are suicidal, there are a myriad of feelings inside that may be overwhelming their ability to sort them out. Identifying the feelings can help focus on what needs to be addressed. If they are frustrated, help them describe what may be frustrating ("I feel like nothing will ever get better"). Or if they are sad, allow them to express what they are thinking about. You can help your loved one create an emotional vocabulary, a list of "feeling" words to help identify what they are feeling. The goal isn't to "fix" the feeling—instead, allow room for them to express it. Having a list to refer to can also help you as you dialogue with them about their feelings.

Know that this may not be a one-time event. Many people with bipolar disorder experience suicidal ideation more times than they report. If your loved one is circling back to this idea, it will be important to create a "contract" with them to not act on their suicidal thoughts. A contract is a simple written agreement you make with the person where they write down that they will not take any action toward suicide and will inform you if they are feeling like they will. It is signed and dated by you and them. Many therapists use this strategy with their clients, and while it isn't a guarantee that the client won't act on the impulse, it helps create an alliance with the client. Bringing the idea of suicide out into the light can take some of its power away from the one it is affecting.

As a caregiver, this cycle of suicide ideation can feel manipulative and frustrating as well as scary and hopeless. Remember, your loved one's brain is not healthy and they need support and care. If it is too much for you, please ask for help from others. Create a plan for what to do when things get difficult for you. It could have the names and phone numbers of the local emergency room, suicide hotline, and your personal support team as well as your pastor or therapist.

And here's one last suggestion: create a safe environment—remove or secure firearms, hunting equipment, and medicine. While you cannot control all possible means of someone harming themselves, take simple steps to secure the obvious threats. If they don't live with you, have a conversation about their home being safe. Talk with them about who they could call or who lives nearby they could connect with when experiencing suicidal thoughts. Encourage them to stay with treatment and to let the professionals they are working with know when they are feeling overwhelmed with thoughts of suicide. These conversations are never easy, and they can be uncomfortable, but they are necessary.

When a Relationship Feels One Sided

How do you manage to stay in a relationship that can be so one sided? Sometimes, the relationship with the person who has bipolar disorder can feel overwhelming and a bit selfish. They may suck the air out of the room, and you disappear, seemingly invisible to the other person. When you begin to feel this way, you might be tempted to address it with your loved one, to clear the air, set the relationship straight.

This isn't a simple question, and it won't have a simple answer. It will depend on what type of relationship this is: child, parent, sibling, spouse, coworker, etc. We will cover this more in the next chapter.

When Safety Becomes an Issue

What if physical and emotional safety becomes an issue? It is a boundary that needs to be firmly established, and if anyone is physically assaulting you, it is not okay, and you need to seek safety. This can be rationalized away with "They didn't mean to hurt me, they have BD, and they were just upset" or "It's not that bad"—but both of those are not helpful to you or the offender. If you are in a physically abusive (grabbing, slapping, shoving, punching, breaking things, punching holes in walls, etc.) relationship, regardless of the diagnosis, you need to ask for help.

This can feel like an overreaction; however, things can escalate quickly, and you need to have a plan of action in place. If it has already happened, create your plan—have money and a key hidden outside of the house, along with phone numbers (friend, pastor, crisis hotline) and a change of clothes. Also, ask someone—a counselor, pastor, trusted family or friend—to help the two of you through this issue. This isn't only for a couple, but any relationship that has become physically harmful. Do not feel embarrassed to ask for help. The person who is harming you doesn't feel good about what they have done yet will repeat the cycle if not helped.

One simple step you can take is to say to the person, "It is not okay to do that. Stop it," and leave the situation. You can also say, "When you are ready to talk, I am willing to listen, but I will not allow you to_____." Make sure you are safe, and if you do not feel safe, please seek safety immediately, or call the police.

Words are sometimes more painful than a punch to the face. If your relationship has become verbally abusive (screaming, yelling, critical, manipulative), you need to make some changes. Unless the house is on fire, or someone is bleeding or dying, screaming isn't necessary. You can decide what you will allow and in what you will participate. If the other person is raging at you, you can say, "I will be glad to talk with you about this issue when you are more calm." Or you can say, "I will not allow you to speak to me this way," and leave the space. The first time you do this, it will feel scary or too confrontational, but you can change the whole situation by drawing this boundary.

You can also revisit the last outburst at a later time. You can address the person by expressing how you felt in that situation, using "I" statements to describe your feelings when the event occurred. You can finish by saying, "I really want our communication to be respectful, honest, and loving," or something similar to affirm that you are trying to make the situation better.

Emotional abuse is just as harmful as physical abuse, except the words are harder to get rid of than the bruises. We usually minimize the damage because we think like the old saying: "Sticks and stones may break my bones, but words will never hurt me." Not only can words hurt, they alter the way we think and function. Regardless of the BP diagnosis, you can decide not to allow raging to become "normal," and if you need to create distance or a boundary in the relationship, whether it's geographically, physically, or emotionally, you can make that decision. The other person doesn't have to be in agreement or even part of your decision. You can decide when and how you will connect with them.

With today's constant communication via text, cell phone, social media, and all other forms, emotional abuse can escalate quickly. You get a phone call from your loved one, and they are raging at you; you feel like you can't hang up. Or they are texting non-stop, and reading the texts is upsetting you. They may do this on a daily basis, but you can decide not to respond to phone calls or texts until you are ready. You can allow the call to go to voice mail. It can feel like you need to respond immediately because of the way the technology creates availability for constant contact. However, you own your device, and you can decide when you will respond to any message or phone call. Not responding to texts immediately, deleting comments on social media, or not answering calls when the relationship has become abusive is a good boundary and can help de-escalate the situation. Let someone know if you are feeling overwhelmed and ask for help.

Geographical boundaries are very healthy when a relationship begins to be destructive. If you have unresolved conflict and it gets reignited when you are with the person, you can decide how much time and space you will spend with the person with BD. Sometimes, that can actually be the catalyst for bringing you closer together in the relationship because you decrease the opportunities for the conflicts to occur. Then over time, the cycle can be broken, and you may even be able to share a meal together without a blowup.

The desperation you may experience as you watch your loved one struggle with different aspects of bipolar disorder is inevitable. When you have just experienced another defeat of hope, remember that you can ask for support as you move forward. It may help to "reframe" the way you are viewing the situation.

Bipolar disorder is life altering, both for the one diagnosed and for those who are in relationship with them. There will be challenges along the way, including new ones that you never thought of before. If you can reframe your thinking from "things will never get better" to something along the lines of "this is part of the journey," it will help you move toward finding help for yourself as well as being an advocate for your loved one.

When You Are Estranged

What if you are estranged from the person with BD? Perhaps you needed to cut all ties from this person for your own well-being. There may still be some guilt, resentment, anger, fear, and grief you are feeling that are unresolved because the relationship was never healed. What then?

When a relationship with a person with BD ends, whether by your choice or by the other person's, you will need to work through the grief and begin to resolve what happened. Accepting the fact that you are no longer in relationship doesn't require you to continue to struggle with the reality. Acceptance doesn't mean agreement or approval; it means that you have understanding, as far as it concerns your part of the relationship, that it has ended. This will free you from replaying the "what ifs" and "should haves" in your mind. It will also enable you to be open to the possibility of a reconnection in the future. Without acceptance, resentment and resistance begin to build, and the likelihood of reconnection is rare.

What about the less dramatic but still difficult issues that occur when in a relationship like this? For example, when you are in a relationship with someone with BD, you will have some really great times together followed by some really low times. Consistent change will be your reality. This doesn't have to be a terrible challenge—if you are flexible and realize that your loved one has a different way of experiencing life. Their brain works differently, and even though you have heard the diagnosis, have seen them comply with treatment regimens, and know the reality, you may struggle with the reality of the relationship.

There are many different scenarios that could be outlined and described here, and it wouldn't begin to scratch the surface of the complexities of relationships—those with BD and not. And you don't have to have the answer for every single situation you will face, but you want to build your resources. Remember to take care of yourself, build your support team, and when you get over-whelmed, ask for help.

The Big Three

There are three basic things that are essential to every relationship. The apostle Paul referred to these in 1 Corinthians 13:13: "faith, hope, and love." You must have faith in the Lord Jesus to equip you with what you need to walk this journey; hope that your loved one will experience relief from the struggle and experience fulfillment in life, including a healthy relationship with you; and love, which Paul describes as being the greatest of the three and which we receive from Christ and can offer to others.

Love is the greatest, and it can be the greatest challenge in this relationship. Knowing when to set a boundary can be the most loving action you take. Recognizing when you need aid as you support the person with BD is loving yourself—which helps you love others. Love enables you to forgive and to accept forgiveness. However, we can have difficulty when we think love does not have boundaries or has difficulty saying "no" or feels bad about sharing its challenges with someone outside this relationship.

Your support system is crucial to expressing and experiencing love. Your support system (friends, family, therapist, pastor, etc.) can remind you that you are loving when you set a boundary, you are loving when you have to say no, and you are loving when you need to take time away from the person with BD. They are on the sidelines offering encouragement, insight, and support to you and your loved one.

Because you have a loved one who is struggling with a disorder, you picked up this book. Your love for them and your hope for the relationship to be healthy and strong are a gift.

CHAPTER 7

When Things Aren't Working

What do you do if you have tried everything and nothing seems to be working? Bipolar disorder changes how relationships function. And the challenge in any relationship is that you cannot make anyone do anything! Even when you want the very best for your loved one and you continue to see them experiencing the struggle of the disorder, the relationship will change.

What does it mean to say, "It isn't working"? Bipolar disorder is not a temporary experience, and those in relationship with the diagnosed can frequently fall prey to the task of "fixing them." You can be supportive and encouraging, and they can decide to reject your help and support. Your intentions can be for their health and welfare—only to have them sabotage your efforts and create more problems. BD is manageable, but the management is primarily in the hands of the person diagnosed. There are many strategies to help them manage, as previously mentioned, but you are not going to be their manager. If you find yourself in this role, that would be an example of things "not working." Our responsibility as loved ones is to offer support, manage our own boundaries, and recognize the difficulty that is sometimes beyond our efforts.

When we think of what is not working in this relationship, it requires a self-assessment of knowing what you can and cannot do for another person. In recovery language, this refers to "tending to your side of the street." If you are continuing to work harder at the care of your loved one than they are, that isn't going to work. The relationship will become codependent and unhealthy.

Elaine shared this about her relationship with her daughter who was diagnosed with BD: "I just know that there will be days when our relationship is enjoyable for both of us, and then other days when it is painful for both of us. But as long as I manage my expectations for her, we avoid many of the power struggles that we used to get into. Seeing her suffer, me wanting to fix her, she wanting me to fix her, her rejecting me ... it was a terrible cycle that lasted too long. Now I trust her to know how to ask me for help, and she knows I am here for her."

How can you have a healthy relationship with someone who is struggling with a mental disorder? We actually do it every day since there are so many people who struggle with mental illness—it's the close and personal relationships that are the more challenging because they are part of our daily lives. Their life intersects with ours in many ways. We can choose to walk away from people we are not in relationship with and go on about our lives. It is the relationships we are in every day, or sometimes just on holidays with family members, that we have to make "work."

How would you describe a healthy, working, functional relationship with the person diagnosed with bipolar disorder? This might be where you describe a good day with this person. What are you currently and consistently struggling with that keeps you from connecting with them? Where do you feel disrespected, dishonored, and uncared for? These questions can help you clarify what you want and need in any relationship and can be helpful as you identify steps moving forward in a relationship with someone who struggles with bipolar disorder.

Trying to discern which parts of the relationship are directly damaged by the disorder and which parts are not can also help repair connection. Healthy detachment is necessary when you recognize you have done all you can do to remain connected and the person is unable to or unwilling to make relationship changes. The challenge is deciphering whether it is the inability due to the disorder or whether they are simply unwilling, which can also be due to the disorder. The decision is ultimately yours if you are able to stay in a relationship, which can be tumultuous and challenging.

When a Spouse Has BD

With each type of relationship, there will be unique difficulties. Some marriages crumble under the weight of bipolar disorder, and while that is unfortunate, it rarely is an easy or rash decision to divorce. Many spouses have tried all they know to do to connect with their spouse who has BD and still struggle with the decision to stay in the marriage. The vows "in sickness and in health" start to reverberate in the thoughts of spouses while the marriage continues to deteriorate. There isn't an easy way to decide to leave a marriage regardless of the issue, and BD is not the exception.

BD, as we have discussed in this book, is not a "curable" disorder. Yes, there can be positive changes, and adjustments can be made; however, some of the issues that are part of the disorder can bring ruin to holy matrimony. Some of the risky behaviors that can occur during mania are extramarital affairs and other inappropriate sexual behavior. This behavior does not automatically have to mean the marriage is over. Some marriages heal from betrayal and can actually be improved from what they were prior to the betrayal. However, repair can only occur when both spouses are focused on and committed to repairing the marriage. If your spouse has been unfaithful due to their BD, you will need a plan for recovery.

One wife explained to me that it was a struggle for her because she kept hoping that the BD was not permanent and that they would someday resume their "normal" relationship. She was hoping this was a "season" in their marriage, and she wanted desperately for the roller-coaster ride to stop. Her expectations kept her from being present with the relationship, which then created tension and resentment along with sadness and loss. Distance was her only relief, but then his behaviors created more separation until the divorce was final. She tried for a decade to resolve the trouble, but her husband was unwilling to accept the challenges and responsibilities of managing the disorder. Letting go of this struggle would be another loss following divorce.

With any marital struggle, regardless of its origin, marriage counseling is an invaluable and necessary step. Having a counselor can help you through the confusion and pain and can help you determine what your next step will be concerning the marriage. You may have been going to some of the therapy appointments with your spouse as part of the treatment plan for the BD. And it is imperative they follow a treatment plan that includes individual appointments. Couples counseling will be focused on your relationship, not just treatment for your spouse's BD. Marriage counseling will be secondary to their therapy, but it can be an invaluable part of the whole treatment process. If your spouse is unwilling to go to marriage counseling, you can invite them to go to express to the counselor their issues with you or what they think is your problem. That may sound offensive, but the goal is to have both of you in the same room with the counselor. Some people are more open to the idea of therapy if they don't feel like it is all about them. If they are still unwilling to participate, go by yourself anyway. To leave a marriage is a big step, and you will need support and your own healing on the other side of the relationship.

Other relationships are not as clear as marriage; you can't "divorce" a child, sibling, parent, etc. How do you manage these relationships? Where do you draw the line?

When a Parent Has BD

With a parent who has BD, you will need to make peace with the fact that they weren't the parent you would have chosen. Forgive them for the challenges you experienced due to their illness. Then move on to gratitude for the life they gave you, and begin the process of accepting that they didn't choose to have bipolar disorder. This is not something that will be done overnight. Take some time to work through the loss, anger, resentment, and forgiveness. Develop a relationship with them based on the present and begin to look for ways to connect in a safe and loving way. Know what your expectations are, and manage them in order to stay present.

Very often, adult children will just move on, away, and avoid any contact with the parent with BD, trying to bury alive the past and the pain of being a child in the confusion and chaos that BD can bring. When we bury anything alive, it will resurrect in other places in our lives. It's okay if you need to create distance from your parent, but make sure you work through your pain and loss so that your choice to distance yourself from the parent doesn't control you emotionally.

One daughter explained to me the challenges of seeing her dad go from her biggest fan when she was an adolescent to disappearing from her life for a while when she was a young adult and then returning years later after her parents' divorce. "One day I decided to forgive him for everything, in order for me to not carry the load any longer. I wrote a letter describing everything that I experienced: sadness, anger, fear, grief, resentment ... and I sent it. I decided to let it go, exhale, and not hold it against him any longer. After a few years, we had dinner together, just he and I. He tearfully and sincerely apologized to me for all that he had done. I was able to honestly say, 'Dad, I forgave you, and I appreciate your apology.'" She went on to describe how their roles had reversed: he was more like a child in the relationship due to his resistance to seek treatment for his BD and his failure to recognize the need for therapeutic help and medication. And when he calls and she recognizes that his thought process is off, like when he wants to go on and on about some minor issue that has nothing to do with anything, she "half-listens and redirects him or ends the conversation." This is her new normal with her dad, and she is doing her best with what she has.

That may not be a possibility for some of you whose parents are no longer alive, but there are still days where you relive some of the chaos of your childhood. Recognize that this is "not working" for you, and seek some supportive help. Work through the grief and loss so that when you think about your childhood, you can recall some good things; forgive your parent and the disorder that created disorder in your life.

When a Child Has BD

When you are a parent of someone with bipolar disorder, you may feel the loss of who you dreamed your child could be, which could possibly make you miss who they actually have become. There is a saying that goes, "Having a child is like watching your heart walk outside of your body for the rest of your life." When you are parenting a child with BD, your heart will be broken, stretched, enlarged, and bruised. You will be challenged as you see their potential get thwarted as a new bipolar cycle begins. The pain and fear will begin to rule the relationship, and you may miss the gifts and talents that they possess and are able to use despite the challenges of BD. You are not alone—others have experienced this.

Some parents have had to mourn the loss of their child with BD due to suicide. The devastation of the loss of a child is overwhelming. Added to this huge loss is the sense that "I could/should have done something more to prevent this from happening." There are no simple words or easy answers to ease the burden or the pain of this great loss. You did all you could do for your child. In order to have some healing of this great wound, you will need support. Do not hesitate to do what you need to get it. When the disorder takes their life, do not allow yourself to be a casualty. Their legacy doesn't have to be just focused on the disorder and the suicide.

You can remember the many other parts of their life, the one that brought joy and love into your life. That is their legacy.

A friend shared this with me: "Parenting a child with BD can take everything you have and more. In my case, my son was extremely cruel in his words to us, his parents. He questioned our love and our motives relentlessly. Their troubled mind creates chaos around them that has the power to disrupt your marriage and the lives of the other siblings. I would encourage parents to spend time with their other children. The time and attention demanded by a child diagnosed with BD is never enough. I'd join a support group of parents dealing with a child with bipolar disorder, especially since most friends and family won't understand what you are going through. Recognize that God understands your love and sacrifice even if others around you don't. Fall back on God's sovereignty and His personal love for you and your child."

When a Sibling Has BD

A sibling may still be at home with you while you are dealing with their challenges. You might feel like they aren't taking up their responsibilities in the family, causing disruption in what otherwise would be a calm household, and you may be fed up with their disorder. It may sound harsh, but for some siblings, this is their reality. They come home to some new drama when they just want the comfort of home. If you are younger than the sibling who has BD, this may not be something new—it may just be "normal" for your household. Your sibling isn't trying to make things difficult for you, at least most of the time. In those times when it is peace-ful, reach out and connect with them; just having a conversation can bring down barriers to your own peace of mind. If, however, you are feeling overwhelmed with what they are dealing with, ask for help from your parents, friends, or counselor or attend a siblings' support group.

Our connection with our adult sibling who has bipolar disorder will most likely be intermittent. Family gatherings, holidays, and celebrations are notorious for drama because we bring old roles with us into these situations. Our expectations go unchecked, and reality greets us with a big slap on the back. If your sibling has been diagnosed with BD, recognize they have challenges that you may never experience and will need some grace. If, however, you have consistently had to deal with personal issues with them, you will have to develop strategies for those times you will encounter them at family functions. Remember not to allow resentment and bitterness toward them to take root in your heart. It will hurt you more than it will affect them. You can only control you, and if you need to create some boundaries—perhaps going to family functions and practicing healthy detachment—it will help you from becoming bitter and resentful.

If you have a sibling who is dependent on you, take extra care to create boundaries and a plan for the relationship. It is a valiant call for you to care for them; however, remember to help them in the areas they are asking for help, and don't take the role of parent (unless, of course, you are the legal guardian). Strategize and create a plan for living together. And with this, you will also have to decide if you are unable to continue if your sibling is unwilling or unable to abide by the plan. Make sure you have your support system, and go to them with your questions, struggles, and challenges. You are not alone even when you feel alone; there is always someone who will listen to you.

Sometimes it is the adult sibling who is still living with your parents who is creating the disruption in the family. It will be helpful to talk with your parents and understand their decision to have your sibling live with them. If there has been a history of violence or alcohol and drug use, let them know they can call you for help. Some adult siblings, living on their own and dealing with their own challenges, may not be interested in a close relationship with you. The disconnect may be difficult for you, or you may secretly have a sense of relief that you won't have to deal with the difficulty of the disorder. Our siblings impact us all, whether they have a diagnosis or not.

When a Friend, Coworker, or Neighbor Has BD

If you have a friend, sibling, coworker, or neighbor who is diagnosed with BD, there will be some built-in boundaries. You probably don't live with them, you can choose to not answer a call or text; and their spending, drinking, and sleeping habits do not directly affect your day-to-day life. That is not saying you don't have feelings about what they are experiencing or the challenges that they are facing. You have probably attempted to help them overcome some of their difficulties, offered solutions or suggestions to assist them, and it has sometimes been successful. In these relationships, the definition of "not working" may be the tension of your trying to help them and the resistance of them following your suggestions.

You might be saying things like "If they would just do_____, they would feel so much better." This phrase can be changed to any part of the help you may have offered: call a particular doctor, read a certain book, go to a treatment center, and so on. It's not that you shouldn't do any of these things. Some of your suggestions may indeed be helpful! The important thing to remember is that everyone gets to make their own choices, even people who have a diagnosis of BD. You can get caught in a web of trying to manage their care when they aren't asking for you to manage their care.

A friend of mine was diagnosed many years ago with BD and has not pursued a regular course of treatment. The medication side effects flatlined what was a formerly energetic and artistic personality. There would be times when I would get a phone call at the depth of the depressive cycle, and we would talk through the desperation. I recognized that our friendship would be different than how it started out, but that is the truth for most friendships. There would be a loss of their home, there would be business and health challenges, but the resilience would allow for a new job and the ability to find happiness and joy in life. We remain friends, and I celebrate the enduring connection we enjoy.

Some of you are in a situation with a coworker who has BD. They may have shared with you the challenges of the disorder and some of their difficulties because of BD. This probably isn't the worst thing to deal with: you can go home after work, and their issues go home with them. The difficult part of this relationship is when/if you are working closely together on a project and they are unable to carry their load due to a depressive cycle, missing work, etc. The challenges of protocol and a healthy work environment and relationship will be pressured. If you are unable to approach them about some options to take when things are difficult, you may need to consult with your manager or human resources. Creating a healthy work environment with mutual respect and understanding is the best approach. People with BD have gifts and talents to share and can be a valuable resource for our workplaces.

A former client once described how difficult it was to go to work during the manic phase. Exhausted from not sleeping and a mind racing with thoughts made it difficult to focus on the tasks at work. The pressure they felt to "keep up good appearances" prevented them from taking time off work. The obvious pressure to pay the bills was also present. They finally decided they had no choice but to leave that career and find something that had some flexibility built in to it.

Understanding that your coworker isn't doing this to you on purpose can be helpful as you seek to find a working relationship. You may be frustrated or irritated; however, do what you can to find common ground. If, however, you find this to be unattainable, you may need to find a different place to work. You might be thinking, *They are creating the problem. Why should I have to get another job?* This is working your side of the street—you can control where you decide to work and whom you will work with.

Our coworkers are a big part of our lives—some of us spend more time with coworkers than with our families! Creating a healthy relationship with a coworker who has been diagnosed with bipolar disorder will be worth the challenges you may face. Recognize when your work or productivity is being impacted, and ask for help, all while maintaining a respectful attitude toward them.

The "not working" part of these types of relationships can be realizing you are trying to control the situation. It can be exhausting to run someone else's life! But you can be involved with them and offer help as they ask. When you offer suggestions, do so with an open hand and heart, allowing them to have the option. If it gets too difficult, when it truly isn't "working" to stay in a close relationship with them, you may need to create some distance—not that you quit loving them or having a presence in their life, but it is a healthy, detached presence. It can feel unloving, but if you become resentful and bitter toward them due to the chaos and conflict in the relationship, the relationship runs the risk of ending completely. Recognize your limits, pray for wisdom, and seek counsel and support from others who can offer help.

Do What You Can

Romans 12:18 reads, "Do all that you can to live in peace with everyone." It doesn't designate who "everyone" is. In *The Message* translation, it reads, "If you've got it in you, get along with everybody." This isn't a directive to be codependent; instead, it addresses the challenges we will all encounter with relationships of any kind. If you are struggling in your relationship with a person who has BD, living at peace with them may be having a good boundary. It may mean disconnecting, respecting their right to deal with the disorder in the way they so choose.

All relationships are teachers. Even when it seems that the relationship isn't "working" due to BD, you are able to learn about how others experience life. It can give you an opportunity to develop compassion, empathy, and perhaps stretch your patience so you can have more for others! We are all flawed, and some of us have a diagnosis that describes our experience of life. However we experience the world and those around us, we have the opportunity to learn from each encounter. We are exposed to our own weaknesses, strengths, gifts, and talents as we interact with others. To try to avoid those whom we might think as too difficult, challenging, or even "imperfect" is to lose the opportunity to grow, learn, and become more aware of the needs around us.

Whether you are married to the person with BD, or whether they are a sibling, friend, or coworker, you will experience the pain of the illness, the relief of stability, and the depth of sorrow—maybe all in the same day. And you don't have the disorder! You will have to make decisions in your relationship to safeguard against unhealthy patterns and behaviors that can become "normal" in this unique relationship. If you are feeling like you are treading water more often than not in this relationship, it isn't working. That does not mean you just quit; as you know, it is not that easy. But you need to pay attention and take action to address the issues.

Recognizing what you expected from the relationship, making peace with the fact they were not or cannot be the person you expected them to be, and forgiving them for the challenges you have experienced as a result of the illness are the steps you need to follow. Begin to recognize some of the things in your relationship with them that you can be grateful for. If you have made the decision to move on, you can still recall some of the better days. If you remain in relationship with them, begin to develop a relationship based on who they are now, utilizing boundaries and self-care and accepting who they are and the gifts they have despite the challenges they face. Seek out support groups; create your support team, which might include a family member, counselor, trusted pastor, and close friend you can call any hour of the day or night. It is worth the effort it will take to make it work—whether you move on or stay in the relationship.

CHAPTER 8

Going the Distance

It is easy to get weary in the journey, to think it will never get any better or to wonder how much worse it will be. While doing research for this project, I ran across many comments in the blogs, articles, and online posts where a loved one of someone diagnosed with BD would respond with rage, sadness, or grief about not receiving the support that they needed or deserved. The person with BD seemed to get a free ticket to just feel however they felt, and everyone around them needed to just accept it and not expect them to get any better. You could almost see the hot tears that would be in their eyes as they would share their pain.

You may be at a stopping point, feeling like there is nothing else that you can do and like you have completely run through your resources. If you feel that way, it is a pretty good indication that you need some self-care, respite, and time to recoup your energy. There will be a thousand reasons you can provide for why you cannot do any self-care. If you are feeling this way and you don't know how to even start the process of self-care, begin with stepping out of the situation. It may be as simple as going for a walk around the block, or it could be more like you need to take the weekend and go check into a hotel for a good night's rest.

Recently, I ran into an old friend. We had lost touch with each other and were catching up. She shared that she had left her husband of thirty-two years, eventually divorced him, saying that he had mental illness. She apologized that she couldn't stay with him any longer, that he had a few incidents that were life threatening to her and her family. "God bless those that can stay. I just couldn't any longer, and I couldn't put my children at risk." The decision wasn't made quickly or without pain and sorrow.

There is a passage in 1 Peter that says, "Sympathize with each other. Love each other as brothers and sisters. Be tenderhearted, and keep a humble attitude. Don't repay evil for evil. Don't retaliate with insults when people insult you. Instead, pay them back with a blessing. That is what God has called you to do, and he will grant you his blessing" (3:8–9). This encouragement, which may seem more of a challenge when you are dealing with someone who has BD, is for our good. It might seem easier to react in anger and frustration when the drama kicks in. But after the dust settles, you will feel worse. This passage offers self-care steps at the very core of who we are.

"Be strong and courageous, for your work will be rewarded" (2 Chronicles 15:7). This phrase is repeated often through the Old Testament to encourage those who were struggling through many different challenges that they feared would overtake them. It applies to your journey as well. The Lord will provide the strength you will need during times when you think you have no more to give. You will be more courageous than you ever thought possible when you face scary decisions and experiences with your loved one. The same strength and courage will be at work when you are setting boundaries, making a bold move, and sometimes even when you are just making a small step in the right direction. The strength and courage you have in this challenging relationship may surprise you.

"What does not kill me makes me stronger" may sound like an encouraging thought, but the jury is still out on this idea. Some of you have been under so much stress and pressure with this relationship that it may be too much. You may be asking, "How much more can I take?" If you are in an abusive situation, or if you even think it may feel abusive, talk with someone. Many people suffer in silence, but there is support available. Remember that your own oxygen mask goes on first!

Don't lose your own voice or betray your own convictions. Relationships affect our lives, sometimes negatively. You may be feeling pressured to go along with things that you don't agree with. Be courageous enough to use your strength to leave the situation if you need to. Needing help or assistance doesn't make you weak, and walking away for a period of time to get your own healing can provide a new perspective and renewed vigor to either love or leave.

It takes courage just to think about those choices, especially when you have been working toward a successful resolution to the challenges you have faced with your loved one. You just need enough strength to take one step, even though that can feel overwhelming. In a relationship that is challenged with BD, the next step can sometimes feel like a loaded decision. "If I leave, how will they take care of themselves?" "I can't take any time (or money) for therapy; they are the ones who need it." "If I set a boundary, there will be hell to pay." There are too many pressure points to make the decision—it feels like a loaded shotgun—the spread will go everywhere. When you are feeling stuck in the process of self-care, take a courageous step and say to yourself, "It doesn't all rest on this decision." It is just one decision.

There will be changes when we make decisions; however, isn't that what we want? We don't want to have things stay the same; we want to change the circumstances and to search for the possibility of better days. It has been said throughout this project that you will need to create a support team of people who speak life into yours. When you are feeling discouraged and overwhelmed with the next right decision, you can ask your support team for … support! That may be the most courageous move you make and could make all the difference in your world.

Everyone is struggling with something. When you are in relationship with someone with BD, you may feel like the rest of the world is carefree and you are the only one facing this difficulty. This isn't a result of you not doing something right, not finding the right doctor or treatment center. This is part of the imperfect world we live in, and we all need help now and then. Make the choice to seek supportive relationships, to practice self-care daily, and to know when you cannot continue in the relationship any longer.

Wishful thinking is when we hope for our reality to be something other than what it is. It can keep us focused on something that may never be part of our reality and can distract us from the present. We can get tired from wishing things would get better instead of getting tired from exercising our choices to find a better reality. Accepting what is and looking for possibilities and being courageous to take the risks for a better today will be the better choice.

Hopefully you have gained some insight into understanding and loving the person in your life with BD. Knowledge can be a powerful tool when you are working on relationship challenges. When you are searching for answers to the challenges that bipolar disorder brings to relationships, remember the first question to ask might be "What do I need?" We can get so focused on helping the other person that we forget that we have to take care of ourselves, which can actually end up being the best thing toward taking care of others!

What is your next step? As you have read through this book, what resonated with you? Maybe your next step is to sit with a friend, counselor, or pastor and share your journey, tell your story. We are often so far in the trenches that we are not aware of what is really happening in our lives. Begin with taking an assessment of your relationship, your own experience in the relationship, and the resources you have. Only when you know where you are can you have an idea of where you want to go. If you have ever been lost and are asking for directions, usually the first question you are asked is "Where are you?" Only when your helper knows where you are can they offer insight into how to get where you want to go. Your story, your experience, makes all the difference in finding a path to freedom.

There is a passage in the Old Testament book of Daniel in which Daniel had been in mourning and described as seeing a man in a vision who said to him, "Don't be afraid ... for you are very precious to God. Peace! Be encouraged! Be strong!" (Daniel 10:19). This is the same thing I would say to you if we were sitting together. You are precious to God, and He sees the challenges you face in your relationship. He knows the struggle your loved one faces with BD. And He will provide the insight and hope you need for your journey.

Be encouraged: you are not alone and without resources. It may seem like you have exhausted the resources and you have no one to turn to, but don't give up. At the end of that story in Daniel, after he hears what the man says, Daniel responds, "You have strengthened me" (Daniel 10:19). You may not have all of the answers to the questions and struggles you face right now, but that doesn't mean forever. Each day offers a new opportunity for new discovery or rest from the search.

As you and your loved one continue on this journey with bipolar disorder, "I am certain that God, who began the good work within you, will continue his work until it is finally finished" (Philippians 1:6).

Notes

Chapter 2: What You're All Experiencing

1. "Bipolar Disorder," Mayo Clinic, accessed June 4, 2018, www.mayoclinic.org/diseases-conditions/bipolar-disorder/basics/symptoms/con-20027544.

2. "Burden," CDC, accessed June 4, 2018, www.cdc.gov/mentalhealth/basics/burden.htm.

3. "Bipolar Disorder," Mayo Clinic, accessed June 4, 2018, www.mayoclinic.org/diseases-conditions/bipolar-disorder/basics/symptoms/con-20027544.

4. "Bipolar Disorder Statistics," Bipolar Lives, accessed June 4, 2018, www.bipolar-lives.com/bipolar-disorder-statistics.html.

5. "Burden," CDC, accessed June 4, 2018, www.cdc.gov/mentalhealth/basics/burden.htm.

Chapter 3: Embracing Empathy for Your Loved One

1. "Causes of Bipolar Disorder," WebMD, accessed June 4, 2018, www.webmd.com/bipolar-disorder/guide/bipolar-disorder-causes.

2. Susan L. Ruth, "Celebrities, Like Robin Williams, with Depression and Bipolar Disorder," CDN, August 14, 2014, www.commdiginews.com/health-science/health/five-celebrities-besides-robin-williams-with-bipolar-disorder-23601/#11xS3KIyKSZxlRsf.99.

3. Jane Pauley, *Skywriting: A Life Out of the Blue* (New York: Random House, 2004).

4. Julia Bhatia, "Thirteen Famous People with Bipolar Disorder," Everyday Health, April 11, 2018, www.everydayhealth.com/bipolar-disorder-pictures/famous-people-with-bipolar-disorder.aspx#02.

5. Natalie Umansky, "Ten Famous People Who Were Bipolar," Oddee, July 18, 2013, www.oddee.com/item_98650.aspx.

6. Lindsay Holmes and Abigail Williams, "A Reminder That Carrie Fisher Was an O.G. Mental Health Hero," HuffPost, October 22, 2015, www.huffingtonpost.com/entry/carrie-fisher-mental-health-princess-leia_us_562795dbe4b0bce347031e34.

7. "The History of Bipolar Disorder," Healthline, accessed June 4, 2018, www.healthline.com/health/bipolar-disorder/history-bipolar#2.

8. "The History of Bipolar Disorder," Healthline, accessed June 4, 2018, www.healthline.com/health/bipolar-disorder/history-bipolar#2.

9. "Manic Depressive and Bipolar Disorder in an Adult Woman," Potomac Psychiatry, accessed June 4, 2018, www.potomacpsychiatry.com/adult-bipolar-study.

10. "Case Study Peter Graham," St. John of God, accessed June 4, 2018, www.sjog.org.au/pdf/Case%20Study%20-%20Peter%20Graham%202015.pdf.

11. John Watson, "Courtesy" in *The Homely Virtues* (London: Hodder & Stoughton, 1903), 168 (Google Books full view).

12. "Brené Brown on Empathy," RSA, YouTube, December 10, 2013, www.youtube.com/watch?v=1Evwgu369Jw.

Chapter 4: Finding Effective Treatment

1. Merriam-Webster, s.v. "empathy," accessed June 4, 2018, www.merriam-webster.com/dictionary/empathy.

Chapter 5: Loving Them, Loving You

1. Reinhold Niebuhr, "Serenity Prayer," Wikipedia, accessed June 4, 2018, https://en.wikipedia.org/wiki/Serenity_Prayer.

NEWLIFE | Help in Life's Hardest Places

Talking about the things no one else will, to bring healing to those who've lost hope

"*I have been living with my secrets* for 30 plus years while failing time and again to stop and all the while them getting worse. For the first time I have learned more about why it is happening, developing an action plan to change, and creating a network of support."

— *Jack*
Intensive Workshop attendee

When you or someone you love is in crisis, you need a trusted friend to walk alongside you—a helper who's been there and understands, but who also has the training and skill to offer practical help.

New Life Ministries, founded by Steve Arterburn, exists to go into life's hardest places with you.

For over 30 years, we've provided expert answers to people just like you on our call-in radio show, *New Life Live!* We also offer a host of other resources, Intensive Workshops, and referrals to a carefully selected network of counselors.

Visit NewLife.com today to see how we can help, or call 800-HELP-4-ME. We want to hear from you!

About New Life Ministries

New Life Ministries, founded by Stephen Arterburn, began in 1988 as New Life Treatment Centers. New Life's nationally broadcast radio program, *New Life Live!*, began in early 1995. Women of Faith conferences, also founded by Stephen Arterburn, began in 1996. New Life's Counselor Network was formed in 2000, and TV.NewLife.com, the ministry's Internet-based television channel, was launched in 2014. New Life continues to develop and expand their programs and resources to help meet the changing needs of their callers and listeners.

Today, New Life Ministries is a nationally recognized, faith-based, broadcasting and counseling nonprofit organization providing ministry through radio, TV, their counseling network, workshops, support groups, and numerous written, audio, and video resources. All New Life resources are based on God's truth and help those who are hurting find and build connections and experience life transformation.

The *New Life Live!* radio program, still the centerpiece of the ministry, is broadcast on Christian radio stations in more than 150 markets. It can also be seen on several network and online channels.

New Life's passion is to reach out compassionately to those seeking emotional and spiritual health and healing for God's glory. New Life Ministries Resource Center receives thousands of calls each month from those looking for help.

For more information, visit newlife.com.

About Stephen Arterburn

Stephen Arterburn, M.Ed., is the founder and chairman of New Life Ministries and host of the number-one nationally syndicated Christian counseling talk show *New Life Live!*, heard and watched by more than two million people each week on nearly two hundred stations nationwide. He is also the host of New Life TV, a web-based channel dedicated to transforming lives through God's truth, and he also serves as a teaching pastor in Indianapolis, Indiana.

Stephen is an internationally recognized public speaker and has been featured on national media venues such as *Oprah*, *Inside Edition*, *Good Morning America*, *CNN Live*, and *ABC World News Tonight*; in the *New York Times*, *USA Today*, *US News and World Report*; and even in *GQ* and *Rolling Stone* magazines. Stephen has spoken at major events for the National Center for Fathering, American Association of Christian Counselors, Promise Keepers Canada, the Lifewell Conference in Australia, and the Salvation Army, to name a few.

He is the bestselling author of books such as *Every Man's Battle* and *Healing Is a Choice*. With more than eight million books in print, Stephen has been writing about God's transformational truth since 1984. His ministry focuses on identifying and compassionately responding to the needs of those seeking healing and restoration through God's truth. Along with Dr. Dave Stoop, he edited and produced the number-one-bestselling *Life Recovery Bible*.

Stephen has degrees from Baylor University and the University of North Texas, as well as two honorary doctorates, and is currently completing his doctoral studies in Christian counseling. He resides with his family in Fishers, Indiana.

Stephen Arterburn can be contacted directly at SArterburn@ newlife.com.

About Becky Lyke Brown

Becky Lyke Brown, M.S., is a licensed clinical counselor, national certified counselor, and director of the New Life Counselor Network, with over eight hundred mental health professionals nationwide.

She has served in ministry in her denomination and local church for over twenty-five years, in leadership, leading women's ministries, teaching and writing Bible studies, leading groups, and encouraging people to experience God's best for their lives.

Becky was clinical director of the New Life Clinic in Dayton, Ohio, and then became part of the New Life Counselor Network as she began her private practice. She worked with individual adults and married and family clients throughout her career. She has served as a group facilitator at the national New Life Weekend Intensives for over a decade. She now helps with planning and coordinating the weekends and counts it as one of the most gratifying experiences in her career.

Becky and her husband, Bruce, just celebrated thirty-four years of marriage. They have two daughters, a son and son-in-law, and two grandchildren. They enjoy spending time on the lake with their family.

At David C Cook, we equip the local church around the corner and around the globe to make disciples. Come see how we are working together—go to **www.davidccook.com**. Thank you!